Collins

AQA GCSE 9-1
Physics

Jen Randall

Acknowledgements

The authors and publisher are grateful to the copyright holders for permission to use quoted materials and images.

Every effort has been made to trace copyright holders and obtain their permission for the use of copyright material. The authors and publisher will gladly receive information enabling them to rectify any error or omission in subsequent editions.
All facts are correct at time of going to press.

All images ©Shutterstock and HarperCollins*Publishers*

Published by Collins
An imprint of HarperCollins*Publishers* Limited
1 London Bridge Street
London SE1 9GF

HarperCollins*Publishers*
Macken House
39/40 Mayor Street Upper
Dublin 1,
D01 C9W8,
Ireland

© HarperCollins*Publishers* Limited 2024

ISBN 978-0-00-867232-4

First published 2024

10 9 8 7 6 5 4 3 2 1

All rights reserved. No part of this publication may be reproduced, stored in a retrieval system, or transmitted, in any form or by any means, electronic, mechanical, photocopying, recording or otherwise, without the prior permission of Collins.

British Library Cataloguing in Publication Data.

A CIP record of this book is available from the British Library.

Author: Jen Randall
Publisher: Clare Souza
Commissioning: Richard Toms
Project Management and Editorial: Richard Toms and Katie Galloway
Inside Concept Design: Ian Wrigley
Layout: Rose & Thorn Creative Services Ltd
Cover Design: Sarah Duxbury
Production: Bethany Brohm

Printed in India by Multivista Global Pvt. Ltd.

MIX
Paper | Supporting
responsible forestry
FSC
www.fsc.org
FSC™ C007454

This book contains FSC™ certified paper and other controlled sources to ensure responsible forest management.

For more information visit: www.harpercollins.co.uk/green

How to use this book

Each topic is presented
on a two-page spread

Organise your
knowledge
with concise
explanations
and examples

Key points
highlight
fundamental
ideas

Higher tier
content is
highlighted
with a yellow
background
and the
HT logo

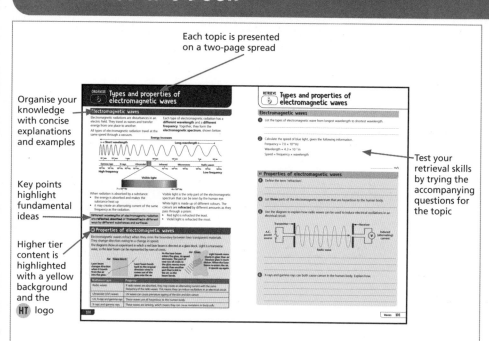

Test your
retrieval skills
by trying the
accompanying
questions for
the topic

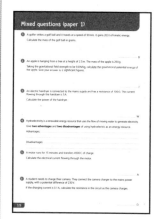

Mixed questions further test
retrieval skills after all topics
have been covered

Scientific and maths skills
sections provide further
knowledge and explanations
of scientific and maths ideas
and investigative skills

Answers are provided to all
questions at the back of
the book

Contents

Contents

1 Energy stores and systems

Energy stores

Energy is never created, or lost, it is just **transferred** between energy stores. This is known as the **law of conservation of energy**.

Suppose a change takes place that causes energy to be transferred from one store to another: if the first energy store decreases by 100 J, the second energy store increases by 100 J.

The five main energy stores are:

Kinetic energy store	Thermal energy store	Chemical energy store
If the cyclist pedals faster, his store of kinetic energy increases.	The poker's store of thermal energy increases when it is put into the fire.	Chemical energy is transferred if the battery is connected into a circuit or if the coal is ignited.

Gravitational potential energy store	Elastic potential energy store	
As the skydiver falls, her store of gravitational potential energy decreases. 	When the archer fires the arrow, the bow's store of elastic potential energy decreases. 	Energy can never be created or destroyed but it can be transferred between different stores.

Energy transfers

Energy can be transferred between the different energy stores by a force, by heating, by an electric current or by a wave.

Whenever you use a domestic appliance that connects to the mains electricity supply, there is an energy transfer by an electric current.	Whenever a force is applied to an object, mechanical work is done and there is an energy transfer by the force.	If an object emits light or sound, there is an energy transfer by radiation. For example, when a lamp is switched on, there is an energy transfer along the electrical pathway transferring energy into the thermal store and into the radiation pathway.

The sequence of energy transfers when a portable gas stove heats water in an aluminium can is shown. The chemical reaction involving combustion of propane and oxygen results in a transfer of energy.

Thermal energy store of aluminium can increases

Thermal energy store of water increases

Thermal energy store of surroundings increases

Chemical energy stored in propane and oxygen → Combustion of propane and oxygen transfers chemical energy to thermal energy → Thermal energy transferred by a temperature difference →

Energy can be transferred between stores by a force, by heating, by an electric current or by a wave.

① Energy stores and systems

Energy stores

1 State the law of conservation of energy.

_____

_____

2 The stem of a pear breaks. The force of gravity acting on the pear causes it to fall from the tree, resulting in a transfer of energy.

a) Name the energy store that is decreasing.

_____

b) Name the energy store that is increasing as the pear falls.

_____

3 A cyclist applies the brakes on seeing a hazard in the road ahead. The force of friction brings the bike to a stop and raises the temperature of the brakes.

a) Name the energy store that has decreased.

_____

b) Name the energy store that has increased.

_____

Energy transfers

4 The incomplete flow chart represents energy changes when a lamp is switched on. Fill in the missing words.

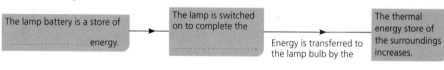

The lamp battery is a store of _____ energy.

The lamp is switched on to complete the _____.

Energy is transferred to the lamp bulb by the _____.

The thermal energy store of the surroundings increases.

5 Describe the energy transfers when a ball is thrown and hits a wall.

_____

_____

_____

_____

_____

_____

1 Changes in energy (1)

Kinetic energy

When an object is in motion, it has energy stored within the **kinetic** store. However, it is not always true to say that the faster an object moves, the greater the energy in the kinetic store. This is because kinetic energy depends on two factors:
- the mass of the object
- the speed at which the object is moving.

The lorry shown below has a mass of 25 000 kg.

The car shown below has a mass of 1200 kg.

Even though the lorry is likely to be moving at a slower speed than the car, it might have more kinetic energy due to its greater mass.

The energy in the kinetic store of a moving object depends on its mass and its speed.

Calculating kinetic energy

You can calculate the energy in the kinetic store of an object using the following equation:

$$E_k = \frac{1}{2}mv^2$$

where

E_k is the kinetic energy, in joules (J)

m is the mass, in kilograms (kg)

v is the speed, in metres per second (m/s)

Sometimes the mass or the speed of the object will not be known, so you will need to rearrange the equation $E_k = \frac{1}{2}mv^2$ to make the unknown quantity the subject. Remember that when rearranging equations, whatever is done to one side must be done to the other.

A lorry with a mass of 25 000 kg is travelling at 15 m/s. Calculate the energy in the kinetic store of the lorry.

Begin by listing the information known about the lorry.

Mass = 25 000 kg

Speed = 15 m/s

Substitute these values into the equation for kinetic energy.

$E_k = \frac{1}{2}mv^2$

$E_k = \frac{1}{2} \times 25\,000 \times 15^2$

$E_k = 2\,812\,500\,J$

If the mass is unknown		If the speed is unknown	
$E_k = \frac{1}{2}mv^2$		$E_k = \frac{1}{2}mv^2$	
$2E_k = mv^2$	Multiply both sides of the equation by 2	$2E_k = mv^2$	Multiply both sides of the equation by 2
$\frac{2E_k}{v^2} = m$	Divide both sides of the equation by v^2	$\frac{2E_k}{m} = v^2$	Divide both sides of the equation by m
		$\frac{\sqrt{2E_k}}{m} = v$	Take the square root of both sides of the equation

The energy in the kinetic store of a moving object can be calculated by $E_k = \frac{1}{2}mv^2$

1 Changes in energy (1)

Kinetic energy

1 State the **two** factors that determine the energy within the kinetic store of a moving object.

2 A bus and a car are both moving at a speed of 20 m/s. The bus has a mass of 15 000 kg and the car has a mass of 1100 kg.

Without calculation, state and explain which object will have the greater kinetic energy.

Calculating kinetic energy

3 A cyclist and their bike have a combined mass of 100 kg and are travelling at a speed of 7 m/s.

Calculate the kinetic energy of the cyclist and bike. Remember to state the unit.

4 A train has a mass of 30 000 kg and is travelling at a speed of 56 m/s.

Calculate the kinetic energy of the train in kilojoules.

.... kJ

5 A rugby player runs at a speed of 4 m/s and has 640 J of energy in the kinetic store.

Calculate the mass of the rugby player in kilograms.

.... kg

6 A Boeing 747 aeroplane has a mass of 184 000 kg and has 5 750 000 000 J of energy in its kinetic store.

Calculate the speed of the aeroplane in metres per second.

.... m/s

1 Changes in energy (2)

Elastic potential energy

When a spring is stretched, it has energy stored within the **elastic potential energy** store. The amount of energy stored depends on two factors:
- how stiff the spring is
- how far the spring extends from its original length – the **extension**.

The stiffness of a spring is given a value, known as the **spring constant**, k. It is defined as the force required to stretch the spring by 1 m.

The elastic potential energy can be calculated using the following equation:

$$\text{Elastic potential energy} = \frac{1}{2} \times \text{spring constant} \times \text{extension}^2$$
$$E_e = \frac{1}{2}ke^2$$

where E_e is the elastic potential energy, in joules (J)
k is the spring constant, in newtons per metre (N/m)
e is the extension, in metres (m)

The spring has a spring constant of 150 N/m and extends by 2 cm.
Calculate the elastic potential energy stored in the spring.

$E_e = \frac{1}{2}ke^2$

$E_e = \frac{1}{2} \times 150 \times 0.02^2$ Remember to convert the extension of the spring into metres.

$E_e = 0.03\,J$

Elastic potential energy depends on the spring constant and the extension of the spring. It can be calculated using the equation $E_e = \frac{1}{2}ke^2$

Gravitational potential energy

When an object is raised above the Earth's surface, it gains **gravitational potential energy**, E_p. The amount of gravitational potential energy gained by an object depends on three factors:
- the **mass** of the object
- the **gravitational field strength**
- the **height** the object is raised to.

The gravitational field strength is the force of gravity per unit mass, measured in newtons per kilogram, N/kg.

The **gravitational potential energy** can be calculated using the following equation:

$$\text{Gravitational potential energy} = \text{mass} \times \text{gravitational field strength} \times \text{height}$$
$$E_p = mgh$$

The summit of Mount Snowdon in Wales is 1085 m above sea level.

Calculate the gravitational potential energy gained by a mountaineer with a mass of 70 kg when they reach the summit of Mount Snowdon. Take the gravitational field strength, g, to be 10 N/kg.

$E_p = mgh$
$E_p = 70 \times 10 \times 1085$
$E_p = 759\,500\,J = 759.5\,kJ$

Gravitational potential energy depends on the mass, the gravitational field strength and the height. It can be calculated using the equation $E_p = mgh$

1 Changes in energy (2)

Elastic potential energy

1 State the **two** factors that elastic potential energy depends on.

....

....

2 A spring has a spring constant of 300 N/m. When a force is applied, it extends by 5 cm.

Calculate the elastic potential energy stored in the spring.

.... J

3 A spring has a spring constant of 500 N/m. When a force is applied, it extends from 5 cm to 25 cm.

Calculate the elastic potential energy stored in the spring.

.... J

4 A stretched spring stores 20 J of elastic potential energy when it extends by 40 cm.

Calculate the spring constant, **k**, of the spring in N/m.

.... N/m

Gravitational potential energy

5 State the **three** factors that gravitational potential energy depends on.

....

....

....

6 A book of mass 0.75 kg is placed on a table that is 1.2 m high.

Calculate the gravitational potential energy gained by the book. Take g to be 10 N/kg.

.... J

7 A golf ball has a mass of 45 g.

Calculate the gravitational potential energy gained by the golf ball when it is hit 20 m into the air. Take g to be 10 N/kg.

.... J

8 A mountaineer of mass 75 kg gains 637.5 kJ of gravitational potential energy when they climb a mountain.

Calculate the height of the mountain that they climb. Take g to be 10 N/kg.

.... m

① Energy changes in systems

Specific heat capacity

Have you ever walked on a beach and felt the heat of the sand on your feet? What do you feel as your feet touch the water?

The water feels much cooler than the sand, despite them both having been under the same Sun. This is because sand and water have very different specific heat capacities.

The **specific heat capacity** is a measure of how much energy it takes to raise the temperature of 1 kg of a particular material by 1°C.

> The specific heat capacity is the energy required to raise the temperature of 1 kg of a substance by 1°C.

Calculating changes in energy

The amount of energy required to heat up a substance depends on three factors:

- the mass of the substance being heated
- the specific heat capacity of the substance being heated
- the change in temperature.

You can use the following equation to calculate the amount of energy required to heat up a substance:

$$\Delta E = mc\Delta\theta$$

where

ΔE is the change in thermal energy, in joules (J)

m is the mass, in kilograms (kg)

c is the specific heat capacity, in joules per kilogram per degree Celsius (J/kg°C)

$\Delta\theta$ is the change in temperature, in degrees Celsius (°C)

An aluminium block has a mass of 1.5 kg.

Calculate the energy required to raise the temperature of this block from 15°C to 35°C. The specific heat capacity of aluminium is 900 J/kg°C.

Begin by listing the information known about the block.

Mass = 1.5 kg
Specific heat capacity = 900 J/kg°C
Change in temperature = (35 − 15) = 20°C

Substitute these values into the equation for change in energy.

$\Delta E = mc\Delta\theta$
$\Delta E = 1.5 \times 900 \times 20$
$\Delta E = 27\,000\,\text{J}$

Sometimes the mass, the change in temperature or the specific heat capacity of the object will not be known, so you will need to rearrange the equation $\Delta E = mc\Delta\theta$ to make the unknown quantity the subject. Remember that when rearranging equations, whatever is done to one side must be done to the other.

If the mass is unknown		If the change in temperature is unknown		If the specific heat capacity is unknown	
$\Delta E = mc\Delta\theta$		$\Delta E = mc\Delta\theta$		$\Delta E = mc\Delta\theta$	
$\dfrac{\Delta E}{(c\Delta\theta)} = m$	Divide both sides of the equation by $(c\Delta\theta)$	$\dfrac{\Delta E}{(mc)} = \Delta\theta$	Divide both sides of the equation by (mc)	$\dfrac{\Delta E}{(m\Delta\theta)} = c$	Divide both sides of the equation by $(m\Delta\theta)$

> The energy needed to heat a substance depends on the mass of the substance, its specific heat capacity and the change in temperature. It is calculated using the equation $\Delta E = mc\Delta\theta$.

1 Energy changes in systems

Specific heat capacity

1 What is meant by the term 'specific heat capacity'?

....

....

2 State the **three** factors that affect the amount of energy needed to heat up a substance.

....

....

....

Calculating changes in energy

3 A copper coin has a mass of 3.5 g. The specific heat capacity of copper is 385 J/kg°C.

Calculate the change in energy of the coin when it is heated from 20°C to 50°C.
Give your answer to 3 significant figures and remember to state the unit.

....

4 Calculate the change in energy when 2 kg of water is heated from 18°C to 100°C.
Give your answer in kilojoules. The specific heat capacity of water is 4200 J/kg°C.

.... kJ

5 An aluminium block is heated from 15°C to 50°C. 78750 J of energy is supplied to the block.
The specific heat capacity of aluminium is 900 J/kg°C.

Calculate the mass of the aluminium block in kilograms.

.... kg

6 A bar of steel of mass 1.5 kg is heated using 28.35 kJ of energy.
The specific heat capacity of steel is 420 J/kg°C.

Calculate the change in temperature of the steel bar.

.... °C

1 Power and energy transfer

Power

An electrical appliance transfers energy stored in the mains electrical supply to other energy stores. When you switch on an electric kettle, an electric current flows through its heating element, transferring energy from the mains.

The energy transfer increases the thermal energy stores of the water in the kettle, the body of the kettle, and its surroundings.

The **power** of an electrical appliance is the energy it transfers in 1 second.

1 joule of energy transferred in 1 second represents a power of 1 watt, written as 1 W.

Household electrical appliances are labelled with their power. If the label on a hairdryer shows that its power is 800 W, this means that it transfers 800 J of energy from the mains supply every second.

> The power of an electrical appliance is the energy it transfers in 1 second. 1 joule of energy transferred in 1 second represents a power of 1 watt (1 W).

Calculating energy transfer

The energy transferred by a device can be calculated using the following equation:

$$\text{power (W)} = \frac{\text{energy (J)}}{\text{time (s)}}$$

This equation can be rearranged to

energy (J) = power (W) × time (s)

Work done is equal to energy transferred, so:

$$\text{power (W)} = \frac{\text{work done (J)}}{\text{time (s)}}$$

If an 800 W hairdryer is used for 5 minutes, how much energy will it transfer?

First convert 5 minutes into seconds

Time = 5 × 60 = 300 s

Now use the energy equation

Energy transferred = 800 × 300 = 240 000 J

Appliances designed to produce thermal energy usually have greater powers. High powers are often given in kilowatts (kW). For example, the power of an iron may be given as 2.4 kW.

> The power can be calculated using the equations:
>
> $$\text{power (W)} = \frac{\text{energy (J)}}{\text{time (s)}} \quad \text{and}$$
>
> $$\text{power (W)} = \frac{\text{work done (J)}}{\text{time (s)}}$$

1 Power and energy transfer

Power

1 Complete the following sentence.

An energy transfer of 1 _____ per _____ is

equal to a power of 1 _____.

2 Two electric motors, A and B, lift the same weight through the same height.

Motor A takes 3 seconds to lift the weight. Motor B takes 10 seconds to lift the same weight through the same height.

Which motor is more powerful? Explain your answer.

_____

_____

_____

Calculating energy transfer

3 An electric immersion heater transfers 10 000 000 J in 20 minutes.

a) Calculate the power of the immersion heater in watts.

_____ W

b) Convert your answer in part a) to kilowatts.

_____ kW

4 The power rating on an electric kettle is 2500 W.

a) Explain what this means in terms of how quickly it transfers energy.

_____

b) The kettle full of water takes 3 minutes to boil.

Calculate how much energy is transferred by the kettle during the 3 minutes it takes to boil the water. Give your answer in kilojoules.

_____ kJ

5 The engines in a train have a combined power of 2 MW.

a) Convert the power of the engines into watts. Give your answer in standard form.

_____ W

b) Calculate the energy transferred by the train over a 30-minute journey, assuming that the engines run at full power for the duration of the journey. Give your answer in MJ.

_____ MJ

1 Energy transfers in a system

Law of conservation of energy

The **law of conservation of energy** states that energy cannot be created or destroyed. Energy can be transferred between different stores, but the total energy in a system remains constant.

If a model car is pushed and then allowed to come to a stop, there is an energy transfer from the kinetic store of the car to the thermal store of the surroundings as work is done by friction in bringing the car to a stop.

The total energy within this system remains constant. In other words, there is no net change in total energy.

When devices transfer energy, only part of the energy is usefully transferred to where it is wanted and in the form that is wanted. The remaining energy is **transformed** in a non-useful way, mainly as thermal energy. This is known as wasted energy.

For example, a light bulb transforms electrical energy into useful light energy. However, for some light bulbs, most of the energy is wasted as heat energy.

The wasted energy and the useful energy are eventually transferred to their surroundings, which become warmer. It is said that the energy has been **dissipated**.

> Energy cannot be created or destroyed. It can only be transferred from one store to another.

Reducing unwanted energy transfers

It is not possible to completely prevent unwanted energy transfers, but you can reduce them.

Where two surfaces rub together, there is always an energy transfer into the thermal store of the objects. **Lubricating** the surfaces (using oil or graphite) reduces friction and therefore reduces the energy transfer into the thermal store.

Applying oil to a bicycle chain reduces the energy transfer to the thermal store, meaning that more energy is transferred into the kinetic store. This increases the speed for the same energy input.

Buildings can be **insulated** with **thermal insulation** to reduce unwanted energy transfers. Cavity wall insulation and loft insulation can be used to prevent heat loss through the walls and roofs of houses.

Cavity wall insulation is made of a material containing pockets of trapped air that is injected into the gaps between the interior and exterior walls of houses. This reduces heat loss via conduction and convection.

Loft insulation is made from a material with a low **thermal conductivity**. This means that the material is a poor conductor of heat, therefore insulating the building.

The rate of cooling of a building depends on both the **thickness** and **thermal conductivity** of the walls. Thick walls, insulated with a material with a low thermal conductivity, have the slowest rate of heat loss.

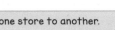
Applying oil to a bike chain

Cavity wall insulation

Loft insulation

> Unwanted energy transfers can be reduced, for example through lubrication and the use of thermal insulators. Effective thermal insulators have a low thermal conductivity.

(1) Energy transfers in a system

Law of conservation of energy

1 State the law of conservation of energy.

2 When a television is turned on, there are useful and wasted energy transfers.

Identify **one useful** and **one wasted** energy transfer.

Reducing unwanted energy transfers

3 It is important to ensure that the oil in a car engine is always topped up.

Explain why oiling moving parts reduces unwanted energy transfers.

4 State **two** ways in which unwanted energy transfers can be reduced in the home.

5 Thermal conductivity is a measure of the rate at which heat energy passes through a material. The higher the thermal conductivity of a material, the greater the rate of energy transfer through the material.

Use this information to explain why loft insulation is made of a material with low thermal conductivity.

(1) Efficiency

Efficiency and how it is calculated

Devices are designed to waste as little energy as possible. This means that more energy can be usefully transferred.

The **efficiency** of a device is the proportion of energy that is usefully transformed. The greater the proportion of energy that is usefully transformed, the more efficient the device is.

The efficiency of a device can be calculated using the equations below. Note that power is a measure of the rate of energy transfer.

Wasted energy Heat 150 joules/s

Useful energy Light 20 joules/s

Useful energy Sound 30 joules/s

Electrical energy 200 joules/s

If a quarter of the energy supplied to a television is usefully transformed into light and sound, it is only 25% efficient.

The total energy supplied to a light bulb is 200J. The bulb usefully transfers 105J of energy. Calculate the efficiency of the light bulb.

Begin by listing the information known about the energy transfer

Total input energy transfer = 200J
Useful output energy transfer = 105J

Substitute these values into the equation for efficiency

$$\text{efficiency} = \frac{\text{useful output energy transfer}}{\text{total input energy transfer}}$$

$$\text{efficiency} = \frac{105J}{200J}$$

$$\text{efficiency} = 0.525$$

Notice that efficiency does not have any units. This is because the units of joules (or watts) cancel out on the top and the bottom of the fraction

---

$$\text{efficiency} = \frac{\text{useful output energy transfer}}{\text{total input energy transfer}}$$

$$\text{efficiency} = \frac{\text{useful power output}}{\text{total power input}}$$

A hairdryer has a power rating of 2000W. It usefully transfers energy at a rate of 1400W. Calculate the percentage efficiency of the hairdryer.

Calculate the efficiency of the hairdryer by $\frac{\text{useful power output}}{\text{total power input}}$ and multiply by 100%

$$\text{percentage efficiency} = \frac{1400}{2000} \times 100\%$$

$$\text{percentage efficiency} = 70\%$$

Rearranging the efficiency equation

If the useful output energy transfer is unknown	If the total input energy transfer is unknown
$\text{efficiency} = \dfrac{\text{useful output energy transfer}}{\text{total input energy transfer}}$	$\text{efficiency} = \dfrac{\text{useful output energy transfer}}{\text{total input energy transfer}}$
Multiply both sides of the equation by the total input energy transfer	Multiply both sides of the equation by the total input energy transfer
$\text{efficiency} \times \text{total input energy transfer} = \text{useful output energy transfer}$	$\text{efficiency} \times \text{total input energy transfer} = \text{useful output energy transfer}$
	Divide both sides of the equation by the efficiency
	$\dfrac{\text{useful output energy transfer}}{\text{efficiency}} = \text{total input energy transfer}$

Increasing the efficiency of a device

Devices can't have an efficiency greater than 1 or 100%. This would mean that more useful energy was transferred by the device than was put into it, breaking the law of conservation of energy.

Energy can be lost due to friction between moving parts, unwanted sound output or by electrical resistance. **Lubricating** moving parts and using thermal **insulation** can reduce the unwanted energy transfers and therefore increase the efficiency of a device.

(1) Efficiency

Efficiency and how it is calculated

1 What is meant by the 'efficiency' of a device?

2 Explain why the efficiency of a device can never be greater than 1.

3 An electric motor usefully transfers energy at a rate of 6W. The input power of the motor is 15W. Calculate the efficiency of the motor.

4 300J of energy are supplied to an LED bulb. The bulb usefully transfers 240J of energy via the radiation pathway.
Calculate the efficiency of the LED bulb.

Rearranging the efficiency equation

5 A television has an efficiency of 0.80 and it usefully transfers 5500J of energy.
Calculate the total input energy transfer.

_____ J

Increasing the efficiency of a device

6 A kettle has an efficiency of 0.75
How could the efficiency of the kettle be increased?

National and global energy resources

Energy resources on Earth

Humans use energy resources for transport, generating electricity and heating.

Some of these resources are **renewable**. This means that they are being, or can be, replenished as they are used. Others are **non-renewable** because they can't be replaced within a lifetime and will eventually run out.

Nuclear fuels such as uranium and plutonium are non-renewable. Nuclear fuel isn't burned like coal, oil or gas to release energy and it isn't classed as a fossil fuel.

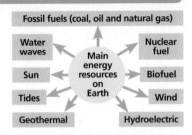

Non-renewable energy resources

Source	Advantages	Disadvantages
Coal	• Relatively cheap and easy to obtain. • Coal-fired power stations have a relatively quick start-up time. • There may be over a century's worth of coal left.	• Burning produces CO_2 and SO_2. • Produces more CO_2 per unit of energy than oil or gas does. Removing the SO_2 is costly. • SO_2 causes **acid rain**.
Oil	• Relatively easy to find, though the price is variable. • Oil-fired power stations are flexible in meeting demand. • There is enough left for the short-medium term.	• Burning produces CO_2 and SO_2. • Produces more CO_2 per unit of energy than gas. • Tankers pose the risk of **spillage** and **pollution**.
Gas	• Gas-fired power stations have the quickest start-up time. • There is enough left for the short-medium term. • Doesn't produce SO_2.	• Burning produces CO_2 (although it produces less per unit of energy than coal or oil). • Expensive pipelines and networks are often required to transport it.
Nuclear	• Cost and rate of fuel is relatively low. • Nuclear power stations are flexible in meeting demand. • Doesn't produce CO_2 or SO_2.	• Waste can stay **dangerously radioactive** for thousands of years. • Building and decommissioning is costly. • Longest start-up time.

Renewable energy resources

Many renewable energy sources are 'powered' by the Moon or Sun. The gravitational pull of the Moon creates tides, while the Sun causes evaporation (resulting in rain and flowing water) and convection currents (resulting in winds and waves).

Source	Advantages	Disadvantages
Wind	• No fuel and little maintenance required. • No pollutant gases produced. • Can be built offshore.	• Turbines cause noise and visual pollution. • Not very flexible in meeting demand. • High capital outlay needed to build them.
Tidal and Waves	• No fuel required. • No pollutant gases required. • Barrage water can be released when electricity demand is high.	• They are unsightly, a hazard to shipping, and destroy habitats. • Variations of tides and waves affect output. • High capital outlay needed to build them.
Hydro-electric	• Fast start-up time. • No pollutant gases produced. • Water can be pumped back to the reservoir when electricity demand is low.	• Often involves damming upland valleys. • There must be adequate rainfall in the region where the reservoir is. • Very high initial capital outlay needed.
Solar	• Can produce electricity in remote locations. • No pollutant gases produced.	• Dependant on intensity of light. • High cost per unit of electricity produced.

① National and global energy resources

Energy resources on Earth

1 State **three** energy resources that are available on Earth.

_____

_____

_____

2 Give **two** uses of energy resources.

_____

_____

3 Name the **three** fossil fuels.

_____

_____

Non-renewable energy resources

4 What is meant by a 'non-renewable' energy resource?

_____

_____

_____

5 Give **one advantage** and **one disadvantage** of using coal as an energy resource.

Advantage: _____

_____

Disadvantage: _____

_____

Renewable energy resources

6 What is meant by a 'renewable' energy resource? Give **one** example of such a resource.

_____

_____

_____

7 Give **one advantage** and **one disadvantage** of using wind as an energy resource.

Advantage: _____

_____

Disadvantage: _____

_____

② Standard circuit diagram symbols

Electric circuits

An electric circuit is a complete path around which an electric current can flow.

A circuit contains:
- a cell or a battery of cells
- at least one device that can transfer energy, e.g. a lamp
- wires, called connecting leads, which join the cell to the components of the circuit
- a switch (usually included).

> An electric current needs a complete circuit in order to flow. A break in the circuit will stop the current from flowing.

Circuit diagram symbols

When drawing electric circuits, straight lines are used to represent the electrical wires and standard symbols are used instead of drawing each component.

For example:

The circuit below has been set up in a laboratory.   The circuit diagram for this would be:

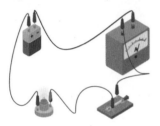   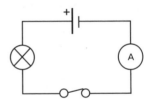

This table shows the symbols that you need to be able to recognise and draw.

Switch (open)	Switch (closed)	Cell	Battery
Thermistor	Diode	Resistor	Variable resistor
Lamp	LED	LDR	
Fuse	Voltmeter	Ammeter	

② Standard circuit diagram symbols

Electric circuits

1 What is meant by an 'electric circuit'?

....

....

2 Write down **four** components of an electric circuit.

....

....

....

....

Circuit diagram symbols

3 Draw the circuit symbols for the following components.

a) Battery

b) Variable resistor

c) Voltmeter

d) LDR

4 Use standard circuit diagram symbols to draw this circuit.

5 Use standard circuit diagram symbols to draw this circuit.

② Electrical charge and current

Electrical charge and current

Electrical current is the flow of electric charge.

The magnitude of the electric current is a measure of the rate of flow of electric charge around the circuit. The greater the current, the faster the flow of electric charge around the circuit.

Calculating electric charge

You can calculate the electric charge and current using the following equation:

$$Q = It$$

where

Q is the electric charge, in coulombs (C)

I is the electric current, in amperes (or amps) (A)

t is the time, in seconds (s)

A current of 10 A flows through a circuit for 5 minutes.

Calculate the electric charge in the circuit.

Begin by listing the information known about the circuit.

Current = 10 A

Time = 5 minutes = 300 seconds

Substitute these values into the equation for electric charge.

$Q = It$

$Q = 10 \times 300$

$Q = 3000\,C$

Rearranging the equation

Sometimes the current or the time will not be known, so you will need to rearrange the equation $Q = It$ to make the unknown quantity the subject. Remember that when rearranging equations, whatever is done to one side must be done to the other.

If the current is unknown		If the time is unknown	
$Q = It$		$Q = It$	
$\frac{Q}{t} = I$	Divide both sides of the equation by time.	$\frac{Q}{I} = t$	Divide both sides of the equation by current.

A circuit transfers 5500 C of electric charge when a current of 5 A flows through it.

Calculate the time the circuit was switched on for.

Give your answer in minutes and seconds.

Begin by listing the information known about the circuit.

Electric charge = 5500 C

Current = 5 A

Resistance = 20 ohms

Substitute these values into the equation for electric current.

$Q = It$

$t = \frac{Q}{I}$

$t = 1100$ seconds = 18 minutes 20 seconds

The electrical charge, current and time are related by the equation $Q = It$

(2) Electrical charge and current

Electrical charge and current

1 What is meant by 'electric current'?

_____

Calculating electric charge

2 In words, write the equation that links current, electric charge and time.

_____

3 A current of 3 A flows through a circuit for 10 minutes.

Calculate the electric charge transferred by the circuit in this time.

_____ C

4 A circuit is switched on for 8 minutes.
A current of 15 A flows through it.

How much electric charge is transferred by the circuit?

_____ C

Rearranging the equation

5 A circuit with a current of 1.5 A transfers 2000 C of electric charge.

How long is the circuit switched on for?

_____ s

6 A circuit is switched on for 15 minutes. During this time, 1200 C of electric charge are transferred.

Calculate the current flowing through the circuit.

_____ A

Current, resistance and potential difference

Current, resistance and potential difference

The current in an electrical circuit depends on:
- the resistance in the circuit
- the potential difference in the circuit.

For a given potential difference across a component, the greater the resistance of the component, the smaller the electric current.

Calculating potential difference

Current, resistance and potential difference are related by the following equation:

$$V = IR$$

where

V is the potential difference, in volts (V)

I is the electric current, in amperes (or amps) (A)

R is the resistance, in ohms (Ω)

Remember that the current is measured in series with the component using an ammeter, and the potential difference is measured in parallel using a voltmeter.

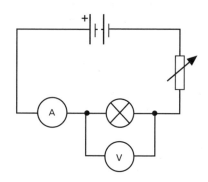

A current of 10 A flows through a circuit with a resistance of 20 Ω.

Calculate the potential difference of the circuit.

Begin by listing the information known about the circuit.

Current = 10 A

Resistance = 20 Ω

Substitute these values into the equation for potential difference.

$V = IR = 10 \times 20$

$V = 200\,V$

Rearranging the equation

Sometimes the current or the resistance will not be known, so you will need to rearrange the equation $V = IR$ to make the unknown quantity the subject. Remember that when rearranging equations, whatever is done to one side must be done to the other.

If the current is unknown	$V = IR$ $\frac{V}{R} = I$	Divide both sides of the equation by resistance.
If the resistance is unknown	$V = IR$ $\frac{V}{I} = R$	Divide both sides of the equation by current.

A circuit with a current of 0.5 A flowing through it displays a reading of 4 V on the voltmeter. Calculate the resistance of the circuit.

Begin by listing the information known about the circuit.

Current = 0.5 A

Potential difference = 4 V

Substitute these values into the equation for electric current.

$V = IR$

$R = \frac{V}{I} = \frac{4}{0.5}$

$R = 8\,Ω$

The electrical current, potential difference and resistance are related by the equation $V = IR$

Current, resistance and potential difference

Current, resistance and potential difference

1 For a constant potential difference, state the effect of the resistance decreasing on the value of the electric current.

....

Calculating potential difference

2 In words, write the equation that links current, potential difference and resistance.

....

3 The total resistance in a circuit is 300 Ω and the current flowing is 0.005 A.

Calculate the potential difference of the circuit.

.... V

4 The current flowing in a circuit containing three resistors is 3.0 A.
The resistors have a combined resistance of 250 Ω.

Calculate the potential difference of the circuit.

.... V

Rearranging the equation

5 The reading on a voltmeter in a circuit is 12 V and the circuit has a total resistance of 4 Ω.

Calculate the current flowing through the circuit.

.... A

6 A circuit with a current of 10 A flowing through it displays a reading of 400 V on the voltmeter.

Calculate the resistance of the circuit.

.... Ω

② Resistors

Resistance

Resistance is a measure of how hard it is to get a current through a component at a particular potential difference.

Current–potential difference graphs show how the current through the component varies with the potential difference across it.

Resistors

For **ohmic conductors**, at a constant temperature, current is directly proportional to potential difference. This means that the value for resistance remains constant as the current changes. This is regardless of the direction that the current is flowing in.

A piece of copper wire is an example of an ohmic conductor. Resistors, such as the one shown in the circuit opposite, are also ohmic conductors.

For **non-ohmic conductors**, the resistance changes when the current changes. LDRs, thermistors, filament lamps and diodes are all examples of non-ohmic conductors.

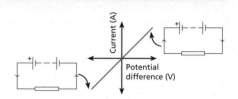

Notice how the line on the graph is a **straight line** that **passes through the origin**. This tells us that the current is **directly proportional** to the potential difference.

For some resistors, known as ohmic conductors, the value for resistance remains constant. For non-ohmic conductors, the value for resistance can change as the current changes.

The resistance of a light dependent resistor (LDR) depends on the amount of light falling on it. Its resistance decreases as the amount of light falling on it increases. This allows more current to flow. This can be useful for switching on lights automatically when it gets dark.	The resistance of a thermistor depends on its temperature. Its resistance decreases as its temperature increases. This allows more current to flow. This can be useful in thermostats, which are used to control the heating in homes.
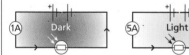	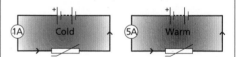
As the temperature of the filament lamp increases, and the bulb gets brighter, then the resistance of the lamp increases. This is regardless of which direction the current is flowing.	A diode allows a current to flow through it in one direction only. It has a very high resistance in the reverse direction so no current flows.
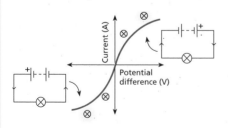	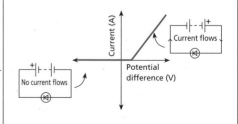

② Resistors

Resistance

① What is meant by the term 'resistance'?

....

....

Resistors

② How can you tell from a graph whether the values plotted against the x-axis and y-axis are **directly proportional** to one another?

....

....

③ Give an example of:

a) an ohmic conductor ....

b) a non-ohmic conductor ....

④ Sketch the shape of a current–potential difference graph for a filament lamp.

⑤ a) Sketch the shape of a current–potential difference graph for a diode.

b) Explain the shape of the graph in terms of resistance.

....

....

⑥ Suggest a use for:

a) a thermistor ....

b) an LDR ....

② Series and parallel circuits

Series circuits

In a **series circuit**, all components are connected one after the other in one loop, going from one terminal of the battery to the other.

The same **current** flows through each component, i.e. $A_1 = A_2 = A_3$.

In this circuit, both bulbs have the same **resistance** so the voltage is divided equally. If one bulb had twice the resistance of the other, then the voltage would be divided differently, e.g. 2V and 1V.

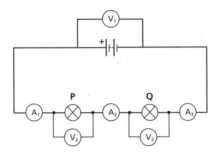

The **potential difference** supplied by the battery is divided up between the components in the circuit, i.e. $V_1 = V_2 + V_3$

The **total resistance** is the sum of the individual resistances of the components, i.e. P + Q. If both P and Q each have a resistance of 15 Ω, the total resistance would be 15 Ω + 15 Ω = 30 Ω

Parallel circuits

In a **parallel circuit**, all components are connected separately in their own loop going from one terminal of the battery to the other.

The total **current** in the main circuit is equal to the sum of the currents through the separate components, i.e. $A_1 = A_2 + A_3 = A_4$.

The **potential difference** across each component is the same (and is equal to the p.d. of the battery), i.e. $V_1 = V_2 = V_3$.

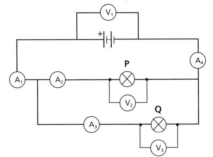

The **total resistance** of the circuit is less than the resistance of the smallest individual resistor. This is because, in a parallel circuit, the current has more paths through which it can flow.

Comparing series and parallel circuits

	Series circuit	Parallel circuit
Current	The current is the **same** through each component.	Total current is the **sum** of the currents through each component.
Potential difference	Total potential difference from the power supply is **shared** between components.	The potential difference is the **same** across each component.
Resistance	The total resistance is the **sum** of the individual resistances of each component.	The total resistance is **less than** the resistance of the smallest individual resistor.

In series circuits, all components are connected in one loop. In parallel circuits, the components are connected separately in their own loop.

② Series and parallel circuits

Series circuits

1 How are the components in a series circuit connected?

....

2 A series circuit is shown. Write down the missing current reading for the second ammeter.

ammeter reads 0.3 A

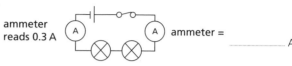

ammeter = ... A

3 Two identical bulbs are connected to a 4.5V battery in series.

Assuming that the bulbs have the same resistance, what will be the potential difference across each bulb in the circuit? Show clearly how you worked out the answer.

.... V

Parallel circuits

4 How are the components in a parallel circuit connected?

....

5 In the circuit shown, two lamps are connected to a cell. The ammeters X, Y and Z measure the current flowing at different points in the circuit.

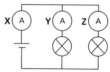

Which ammeter, X, Y or Z, will have the highest reading? Explain your answer.

....

....

....

Comparing series and parallel circuits

6 Complete the table comparing series and parallel circuits by writing the missing words in the spaces.

	Series circuit	Parallel circuit
Current	The current is the .... through each component.	Total current is the .... of the currents through each component.
Potential difference	Total potential difference from the power supply is .... between components.	The potential difference is the .... across each component.
Resistance	The total resistance is the .... of the individual resistances of each component.	The total resistance is .... than the resistance of the smallest individual resistor.

ORGANISE 2 Direct and alternating potential difference and mains electricity

Direct and alternating potential difference

Direct potential difference produces a constant electric current that flows in one direction.

If current or voltage is plotted against time, the graph shows a constant, horizontal line.

Current or Voltage

Alternating potential difference produces an alternating current that regularly changes direction.

If current or voltage are plotted against time for alternating potential difference, you can see the regular change in direction.

Current or Voltage

> Direct potential difference produces a direct current.
> Alternating potential difference produces an alternating current.

Mains electricity

Mains electricity is transmitted by an alternating potential difference supply. This is because the electricity can be transmitted more efficiently this way.

The frequency is the number of complete cycles of reversal per second. The UK mains electricity is 50 cycles per second (hertz). The UK mains supply has a voltage of about 230 volts. This voltage, if it isn't used safely, can kill.

The three-core cable

Most appliances connect to the mains electricity supply using a cable and a three-pin plug. The plug inserts into a socket on the ring main circuit.

The materials used for the plug and cable depend on their properties:

- The inner cores of the wires are made of copper because it's a good conductor.
- The outer layers are made of flexible plastic because it's a good insulator.
- The pins of a plug are made from brass because it's a good conductor.
- The casing is made from plastic or rubber because both are good insulators.

You might be asked to state **where** each wire in the three-core cable should be connected inside a plug.

Remember that:

- the **bl**ue wire is connected to the **b**ottom **l**eft
- the **br**own wire is connected to the **b**ottom **r**ight
- this leaves the green and yellow wire connected in the centre.

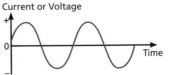

Earth wire (green and yellow)

Neutral wire (blue) – completes the circuit to allow current to flow to the device

Cable grip – secures cable in the plug

Casing

Fuse

Live wire (brown) – completes the circuit to allow current to flow to the device

Cable

Wire	Function
Live	Carries alternating current from the supply to the device
Neutral	Completes the circuit to allow current to flow to the device
Earth	Safety wire; this stops the appliance from becoming live

The potential difference between the live wire and the earth wire is 230 V. The neutral wire has the same potential difference as the earth wire: 0 V. The earth wire only carries an electric current if there is a fault in the appliance. This prevents the appliance from becoming live and therefore very dangerous to touch.

Direct and alternating potential difference and mains electricity

Direct and alternating potential difference

1 What is meant by an 'alternating potential difference'?

....

....

2 On the axes below, sketch the voltage–time graph for direct potential difference.

V

t

Mains electricity

3 Write down the frequency and the potential difference of the mains electricity supply.

Frequency: ....

Potential difference: ....

4 Is the mains electricity supply given by an alternating or a direct potential difference? Give a reason for your answer.

....

....

....

The three-core cable

5 The inner cores of the cables in a three-core cable are made from copper.

Why is copper used?

....

....

6 Complete the table below showing the functions of each wire in a three-core cable.

Wire	Function
Live	Carries .... current from the .... to the ....
Neutral	.... the circuit to allow .... to flow to the device.
Earth	.... wire; this stops the appliance from becoming ....

2 Electrical power

What is electrical power?

The **power** of an electrical device is a measure of the rate of energy transfer by the device. For example, a microwave oven with a power rating of 900W transfers 900J of energy every second that it is turned on.

The greater the power of the device, the faster the rate of energy transfer.

Calculating electrical power

The power of a device depends on the potential difference supplied to it and the current flowing through it. The current, potential difference and power are related by the following equation:

$$P = IV$$

where

P is the power, in watts (W)

I is the current, in amperes (or amps) (A)

V is the potential difference, in volts (V)

Sometimes, the potential difference is not known but the resistance of the device is given instead.

As $V = I \times R$, it can be substituted into the equation for power to give $P = I \times I \times R$

This gives an alternative equation for calculating power:

$$P = I^2R$$

where

P is the power, in watts (W)

I is the current, in amperes (or amps) (A)

R is the resistance, in ohms (Ω)

a) An electric kettle is connected to the mains supply, with a potential difference of 230V. The current flowing through the kettle is 9A. Calculate the power of the kettle.

Begin by listing the information known about the kettle.

Potential difference = 230V
Current = 9A

Substitute these values into the equation for power.

$P = IV = 9 \times 230$
$P = 2070$W

b) An electric hairdryer is connected to the mains supply and has a resistance of 100Ω. The current flowing through the hairdryer is 5A. Calculate the power of the hairdryer.

List the information known about the hairdryer.

Resistance = 100Ω
Current = 5A

Substitute these values into the equation for power.

$P = I^2R = 5^2 \times 100$
$P = 2500$W

Rearranging the equations

Sometimes you will need to rearrange the equations $P = IV$ or $P = I^2R$ to make the unknown quantity the subject.

If the current is unknown		If the potential difference is unknown		If the resistance is unknown	
$P = IV$ $I = \dfrac{P}{V}$	Divide both sides of the equation by V.	$P = IV$ $V = \dfrac{P}{I}$	Divide both sides of the equation by I.	$P = I^2R$ $\dfrac{P}{I^2} = R$	Divide both sides of the equation by I^2.
Or					
$P = I^2R$ $\dfrac{P}{R} = I^2$	Divide both sides of the equation by R.				
$\sqrt{\dfrac{P}{R}} = I$	Take the square root of both sides.				

Electrical power can be calculated using the equations $P = IV$ and $P = I^2R$

② Electrical power

What is electrical power?

1 What is meant by 'electrical power'?

....

....

Calculating electrical power

2 A television is connected to the mains electricity supply, with a potential difference of 230V. When it is switched on, the current flowing through the television is 0.7 A.

Calculate the power of the television.

.... W

3 A vacuum cleaner has a resistance of 35 Ω and a current of 8.45 A flowing through it.

Calculate the power of the vacuum cleaner.

.... W

Rearranging the equations

4 An electric motor has a potential difference of 250V and a power rating of 8kW.

Calculate the current flowing through the motor when it is switched on.

.... A

5 A bulb is connected in a circuit. The current flowing through the bulb is 3 A and the lamp has a power rating of 4.5 W.

Calculate the potential difference of the power supply in the circuit.

.... V

6 A vacuum cleaner has a power rating of 2600 W and a current of 13 A.

Calculate the resistance of the vacuum cleaner. Give your answer to 3 significant figures.

.... Ω

7 A microwave oven has a power rating of 900 W and a resistance of 100 Ω.

Calculate the current flowing through the microwave when it is switched on.

.... A

② Energy transfers in appliances

Energy transfers in everyday appliances

Electrical devices are used to transfer energy. When an appliance is switched on, charge flows around the circuit. When charge flows around an electric circuit, work is done and so energy is transferred.

The amount of electrical energy transferred by an appliance depends on **two** factors:
- how long the appliance is switched on for
- the power of the appliance.

Calculating energy transfer

The amount of electrical energy transferred by an appliance depends on the power and the time it is switched on for. The energy transferred, power and time are related by the following equation:

$$E = Pt$$

where

E is the energy transferred, in joules (J)

P is the power, in watts (W)

t is the time, in seconds (s)

An electric kettle with a power rating of 2200 W takes $2\frac{1}{2}$ minutes to boil when it is filled with water. Calculate the energy transferred by the kettle in this time.

Begin by listing the information known about the kettle.

Power = 2200 W

Time taken = $2\frac{1}{2}$ minutes = 150 seconds

Substitute these values into the equation for energy transferred.

$E = Pt$
$E = 2200 \times 150$
$E = 330\,000\,J$

Sometimes the power or the time will not be known, so you will need to rearrange the equation $E = Pt$ to make the unknown quantity the subject. Remember that when rearranging equations, whatever is done to one side must be done to the other.

If the power is unknown		If the time is unknown	
$E = Pt$ $\frac{E}{t} = P$	Divide both sides of the equation by time.	$E = Pt$ $\frac{E}{P} = t$	Divide both sides of the equation by power.

You know that $E = Pt$

Since $P = IV$, you can substitute this into the equation to give:
$E = VIt$

Since $Q = It$, you can substitute this into the equation to give:
$E = VQ$

where E = energy transferred, measured in joules (J)

V = potential difference, measured in volts (V)

Q = electric charge, measured in coulombs (C)

Energy transferred can be calculated using the equations $E = Pt$ and $E = VQ$

An electric oven, connected to the mains supply at 230 V, transfers 93 600 C of charge over a period of 2 hours. Calculate the energy transferred by the oven in this time. Give your answer in kilojoules (kJ).

List the information known about the oven.

Potential difference = 230 V
Charge = 93 600 C

Substitute these values into the equation for energy transferred.

$E = VQ$
$E = 230 \times 93\,600$
$E = 21\,528\,000\,J$
$E = 21\,528\,kJ$

(2) Energy transfers in appliances

Energy transfers in everyday appliances

1 State the **two** factors that the amount of energy transferred by an electrical appliance depends on.

....

....

Calculating energy transfer

2 In words, write the equation that links energy transferred, power and time.

....

3 A pair of hair straighteners, with a power rating of 60 W, is switched on for 20 minutes.

Calculate the energy transferred by the hair straighteners in this time.

.... J

4 A 1500 W food blender transfers 180 kJ of energy when it is used.

Calculate the time the blender is used for. Give your answer in minutes.

.... minutes

5 A laptop transfers 702 kJ of energy when it is used for a period of 3 hours.

Calculate the power of the laptop.

.... W

6 In words, write the equation that links charge, energy transferred and potential difference.

....

7 A desk lamp, connected to the mains electricity supply at 230 V, transfers 6000 C of electric charge.

Calculate the energy transferred by the lamp.

.... J

8 An electric iron is connected to the mains supply (230 V) and transfers 165.5 kJ of energy in the time it is used.

Calculate the charge transferred by the electric iron.

.... C

9 A bulb is connected to a circuit and, when it is switched on, 150 J of energy are transferred. The charge transfer is 100 C.

Calculate the voltage of the power supply for the circuit.

.... V

② The National Grid

What is the National Grid?

The National Grid is a system of cables and transformers linking power stations to consumers.

The National Grid links power stations to consumers via a system of **transformers** and **cables**. It is only the transformers and cables that make up the National Grid, **not** the power stations and homes.

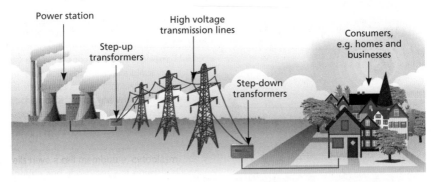

Power station

Step-up transformers

High voltage transmission lines

Step-down transformers

Consumers, e.g. homes and businesses

Parts of the National Grid

Electricity is generated at a potential difference of around 25000V in a power station outside of the National Grid.

Step-up transformers are used to increase the potential difference to around 400000V.

Increasing the potential difference to such high values means that the current through the cables remains very low. This significantly reduces energy loss through heating of the cables, meaning that the transmission is very **efficient**.

Since homes, offices, hospitals and other buildings are usually a long way from power stations, overhead **transmission cables** are used to transmit the electricity from the transformers. Pylons are used to raise these cables high above ground level to keep people safe.

The cables used are very thick to further reduce energy loss through them being heated. This reduces the **resistance** in the cables.

As $P = I^2R$, keeping the current and the resistance low ensures that the power is delivered to the consumer as opposed to being dissipated into the surroundings as heat. However, voltages of 400000V are incredibly dangerous and cannot be used safely in homes and offices.

Step-down transformers are used to decrease the potential difference down to 230V; a safe level if used correctly.

See page 118 for more about transformers.

Step-up transformer

Iron core

Primary coil (input)

Secondary coil (output)

Step-down transformer

Iron core

Primary coil (input)

Secondary coil (output)

Step-up transformers are used to increase the potential difference so that electricity is transmitted at a low current, reducing energy loss by heating.

Step-down transformers are used to decrease the potential difference so that electricity can be safely used by consumers.

2 The National Grid

What is the National Grid?

1 Which of the following accurately describes the National Grid? Tick the correct answer.

A Power stations and transmission cables linked to consumers ☐

B Transmission cables connected to pylons ☐

C Cables and transformers linking power stations to consumers ☐

D Power stations, cables and transformers ☐

Parts of the National Grid

2 What is the function of a **step-up** transformer in the National Grid?

3 Why is electricity transmitted at a voltage of 400 000 V, as opposed to a safer voltage of 230 V?

4 What is the function of a **step-down** transformer in the National Grid?

5 Transmission cables in the National Grid are very thick.

Using ideas about resistance, explain why.

② Static charge

Creating static charge

If you rub a balloon on your hair, it acquires a static charge. This charge is made up of tiny particles called **electrons**, which have transferred from atoms in your hair to the balloon.

- Objects that **gain** electrons are **negatively** charged.
- Objects that **lose** electrons are **positively** charged.

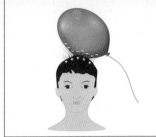

The effect of static charge can be shown by placing the charged balloon just above small bits of paper on a table. An interaction between electrons on the balloon and charged particles in the paper lifts them up off the table. This interaction is an attractive force that works across the space between the balloon and the table.

Forces created by static charges are non-contact forces.

The space around a charged object is called an **electric field**. If another charged object enters that electric field, an interaction will occur.

Imagine one of the charged balloons being surrounded by its own electric field. When the other charged balloon is put into this field, an interaction occurs in the form of a repulsive force.

- Two negatively charged objects **repel** each other.
- Two positively charged objects also **repel** each other.
- A positively charged object and a negatively charged object **attract** each other.

When two electrically charged objects are brought together, they exert a force on each other. This is an example of a non-contact force.

Perspex rod repels a perspex rod

Perspex rod attracts an ebonite rod

Using static charge

Static charge is used to paint cars:

- The body of a car is given a negative charge and is then surrounded by its own electric field.
- The robotic arms control paint spray guns. The paint emitted is positively charged as it leaves the spray gun.
- The car's electric field pulls the positively charged paint droplets towards it, covering the car evenly. Very little paint ends up on the floor.

Static charge also has other uses:

- In factories, electrostatic air cleaners use static charge to remove dust and other particles from the air.
- Photocopiers use static charge to get a black pigment, called toner, to form the text or image being copied on to paper.

② Static charge

Creating static charge

1 When you use a plastic comb on your hair, tiny particles from the atoms in your hair are transferred to the comb. If the comb is placed a few centimetres above bits of paper on a table, its static charge attracts some of them.

a) Name the tiny particles that are transferred from the hair to the comb.

....

b) Does the comb become **positively** or **negatively** charged? Explain your answer.

....

....

c) What name is given to the space surrounding the comb that is affected by its charge?

....

d) The force between the charged comb and the bits of paper is an example of what kind of force?

....

2 When a glass rod is rubbed with a silk cloth, electrons are transferred from the rod to the cloth.

a) Does the glass rod gain **positive** or **negative** charge? Explain your answer.

silk cloth

....

....

b) Two charged glass rods are moved towards each other so that their electric fields overlap. Describe the force between the two glass rods. Explain your answer.

....

....

Using static charge

3 The diagram shows a normal paint gun and its jet of spray. The paint droplets from a normal paint gun are **not** charged. The paint droplets from an electrostatic gun are given a positive charge as they leave the gun.

a) Draw the shape of the jet of spray from the electrostatic paint gun.

b) Explain the shape of the jet you have drawn in part a).

....

....

(2) Electric fields

What is an electric field?

You have seen on pages 40–41 that charged objects create **electric fields** around themselves. An electric field is a region of space within which another charged object would experience a **force**.

Representing electric fields

Electric field around a <u>positively</u> charged object	Electric field around a <u>negatively</u> charged object
Each field line is drawn perpendicular to the surface of the object.	Notice that the field lines point in the opposite direction.
These are called electric **field lines**.	

Electric field lines always point **from** positive **to** negative. This is because the arrows represent the force that a point positive charge would experience if placed in the field. Positive charges would be **repelled** away from a positive object, but **attracted** towards a negative object.

The field lines are **closest together** at the surface of the object and they spread out further away from the object.

Electric fields are strongest close to the charged object and get weaker as the distance from the charged object increases.

> Electric fields are represented by field lines, which point from positive to negative.

Sparking

The concept of electric fields can be used to explain electrostatic phenomena such as **sparking**.

As two surfaces are rubbed together, electrons transfer from one object to another. This leads to a build-up of charge, which in turn leads to a difference in charge between the negatively charged object and the earth.

The earth has a potential of 0 V. As the surface of the object is charged, the difference in charge between the object and the earth increases. Eventually, this difference in charge leads to sparking, where electrons jump from the charged surface to the earth. We see this as a spark.

The greater the charge difference, the brighter the spark.

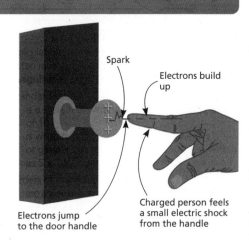

Spark

Electrons build up

Charged person feels a small electric shock from the handle

Electrons jump to the door handle

② Electric fields

What is an electric field?

1 Define the term 'electric field'.

Representing electric fields

2 In the space below, draw a diagram showing the electric field around a negatively charged object.

3 Explain what the arrows in electric field lines represent.

4 Describe the relationship between the electric field strength and the distance from the charged object.

Sparking

5 In terms of electrons, explain the concept of electric sparking.

③ Density

Density and states of matter

Density is a measure of how heavy something is for its size (volume).

In dense materials:
- the particles are close together
- there is very little space between the particles.

Usually, for the same material:
- a gas is less dense than a liquid
- a liquid is less dense than a solid.

Density and states of matter

Gas	Liquid	Solid

Low density   High density

Water is an exception. Liquid water is more dense than solid water (ice). This is why ice floats on water.

Calculating density

The density of a material depends on:
- the mass of the material
- the volume taken up by the material.

Density can be calculated using the equation below:

$$\rho = \frac{m}{v}$$

where

ρ is the density, in kilograms per cubic metre (kg/m³)

m is the mass, in kilograms (kg)

v is the volume, in cubic metres (m³)

A concrete block has a mass of 4800 kg and a volume of 2 m³. Calculate the density of the concrete block.

Begin by listing what is known about the block.

Mass = 4800 kg   Volume = 2 m³

Substitute these values into the equation for density.

$$\rho = \frac{m}{v} = \frac{4800}{2} = 2400 \text{ kg/m}^3$$

To calculate density, you need to:
- measure mass – use a top pan balance to get a value of the mass of a substance
- measure volume.

If the shape is **irregular**, use a Eureka can and a measuring cylinder to measure the volume of the displaced water.

Sometimes you will need to rearrange the equation $\rho = \frac{m}{v}$ to make the unknown quantity the subject.

If the mass is unknown	$\rho = \frac{m}{v}$ $\rho \times v = m$	Multiply both sides of the equation by volume.
If the volume is unknown	$\rho = \frac{m}{v}$ $\rho \times v = m$	Multiply both sides of the equation by volume.
	$v = \frac{m}{\rho}$	Divide both sides of the equation by density.

Floating and sinking

When substances are heated, they expand and their density decreases. So, as air gets heated, the spaces between the gas particles increase and the air expands. This means there are the same number of particles but they take up a greater volume, and so density decreases. The warm air rises. This is how a hot air balloon rises.

A less dense material floats on top of a more dense material.

Cooking oil has a density of 0.93 g/cm³ and water has a density of 1.00 g/cm³, so the oil floats on water.	Sand has a density of 1.5 g/cm³ and so it sinks in water.

③ Density

Density and states of matter

1 What **two** factors does the density of an object depend on?

....

2 Using particle diagrams, explain why the density of a solid substance tends to be greater than the density of the same mass of the same substance in the gas state.

....

....

....

....

....

Calculating density

3 In words, write the equation that links density, mass and volume. Give the units that each quantity is measured in.

....

....

4 A lead block with a volume of 0.1 m³ has a mass of 1134.3 kg.

Calculate the density of the block.

.... kg/m³

5 A gold ring has a mass of 7.5 g. The density of gold is 19 320 kg/m³.

Calculate the volume of gold used to make the ring.

.... m³

Floating and sinking

6 An iron nail is dropped into a beaker of water. The density of water is 998 kg/m³ and the density of iron is 7860 kg/m³.

Use this information to decide whether the iron nail will float or sink in water. Explain your answer.

....

....

Changes of state and internal energy

Changing state

When a substance changes state, only the movement and position of the particles change. This means that changing state is a physical change.

Substances can change state if you add or remove heat (thermal energy).

Energy transferred to the particles from the surroundings by heat

Sublimation

Solid → Melting → Liquid → Boiling → Gas

Solid ← Freezing ← Liquid ← Condensation ← Gas

Energy transferred from the particles to the surroundings by heat

Melting and boiling points

The graph shows the heating of an ice cube.

The temperature increases as you heat the ice until the melting point is reached at 0°C.

The melting point is where a pure substance changes state from a solid to a liquid. At this point, the temperature does not change as all the heat (thermal energy) is being used to overcome the strong intermolecular forces between water particles in the ice.

Once the ice has melted, the temperature rises again until the boiling point is reached at 100°C.

The boiling point is where a pure substance changes state from a liquid to a gas. At this point, the temperature does not change as all the energy is being used to pull the water particles apart to form steam.

The melting and boiling points of an unknown substance can be compared to information on databases in order to identify it.

Temperature (T)

$T_{Boiling}$

$T_{Melting}$

(solid)

(solid + liquid mixture)

(liquid)

(liquid + gas mixture)

(gas)

→ Time

Melting starts | Melting is complete | Boiling starts | Boiling is complete

Evaporation and boiling

Both evaporation and boiling involve changing a liquid into a gas, but they have differences.

Evaporation	Boiling
• Occurs at any temperature between the melting point and boiling point of the substance • Is a slow process • Only happens at the surface • Energy comes mainly from kinetic energy of the substance	• Only happens at boiling point • Whole liquid changes to a gas • Energy comes mainly from the surroundings of the substance

Internal energy

Internal energy is equal to the sum of all of the kinetic energy and potential energy of the particles within a system.

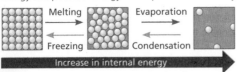

Melting → Evaporation →

← Freezing ← Condensation

Increase in internal energy →

When a substance is heated up, the particles in the system gain energy. This change in energy within the system either:
• causes the temperature of the substance to rise, or
• changes the state of the substance.

③ Changes of state and internal energy

Changing state

1 Complete the diagram by adding the names of the state changes in the answer spaces.

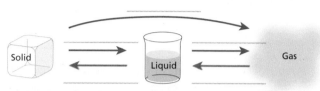

Melting and boiling points

2 **a)** Define the term 'melting point'.

b) Define the term 'boiling point'.

3 Sketch a temperature–time graph for a substance being heated and changing from a solid to a liquid and then finally to a gas.

Label the graph with the melting point and boiling point of the substance.

Evaporation and boiling

4 State **one similarity** and **one difference** between evaporation and boiling.

Similarity:

Difference:

Internal energy

5 Define the term 'internal energy'.

Temperature changes in a system and specific heat capacity

Temperature changes in a system

When the temperature of a substance increases, the extent to which it increases depends on:
- the mass of the substance heated
- the type of substance being heated
- the energy input to the system.

If the same energy were inputted to the water in the beaker and the water in the bath tub, the temperature rise of the water in the beaker would be greater than that in the bath tub, despite water being the substance heated in both cases. This is because the mass of the water in the beaker is significantly less than the mass of the water in the bath tub.

Specific heat capacity

As seen on page 12, **specific heat capacity** is the amount of energy required to raise the temperature of 1 kg of a substance by 1°C. This means that, with the same energy input, some substances will experience a greater increase in temperature than others. The higher the specific heat capacity, the smaller the temperature rise for the same energy input.

Examples of specific heat capacities

Copper	389 J/kg°C
Aluminium	900 J/kg°C
Water	4200 J/kg°C

Calculations involving temperature changes in a system

The input energy, mass, specific heat capacity and temperature change are linked by the equation below:

$$\Delta E = mc\Delta\theta$$

where

ΔE is the change in thermal energy, in joules (J)
m is the mass, in kilograms (kg)
c is the specific heat capacity, in joules per kilogram per degree Celsius (J/kg°C)
$\Delta\theta$ is the change in temperature, in degrees Celsius (°C)

Sometimes you will need to rearrange the equation $\Delta E = mc\Delta\theta$ to make the unknown quantity the subject.

If the mass is unknown	$\Delta E = mc\Delta\theta$ $\frac{\Delta E}{(c\Delta\theta)} = m$	Divide both sides of the equation by $(c\Delta\theta)$
If the change in temperature is unknown	$\Delta E = mc\Delta\theta$ $\frac{\Delta E}{(mc)} = \Delta\theta$	Divide both sides of the equation by (mc)
If the specific heat capacity is unknown	$\Delta E = mc\Delta\theta$ $\frac{\Delta E}{(m\Delta\theta)} = c$	Divide both sides of the equation by $(m\Delta\theta)$

a) A copper coin has a mass of 5.5 g and, when heated, its temperature rises from 15°C to 80°C. The specific heat capacity of copper is 389 J/kg°C. Calculate the change in thermal energy of the coin.

Begin by listing the information known about the coin

Mass $= \frac{5.5}{1000} = 5.5 \times 10^{-3}$ kg
Specific heat capacity = 389 J/kg°C
Change in temperature = 80°C − 15°C = 65°C

Substitute these values into the equation

$\Delta E = mc\Delta\theta$
$\Delta E = (5.5 \times 10^{-3}) \times 389 \times 65$
$\Delta E = 139.1$ J

b) 315 kJ of energy are supplied to a 1.5 kg brick. Brick has a specific heat capacity of 840 J/kg°C. Calculate the change in temperature of the brick.

Begin by listing the information known about the brick

Mass = 1.5 kg
Specific heat capacity = 840 J/kg°C
Change in thermal energy = 315 kJ = 315 000 J

Substitute these values into the equation

$\Delta E = mc\Delta\theta$
$\frac{\Delta E}{(mc)} = \Delta\theta$
$\Delta\theta = \frac{315\,000}{(1.5 \times 840)}$
$\Delta\theta = 25°C$

RETRIEVE 3 · Temperature changes in a system and specific heat capacity

Temperature changes in a system

1 When a substance is heated with no change of state, its temperature will rise.

State the **three** factors that this size of temperature rise will depend on.

....

....

....

Specific heat capacity

2 Define the term 'specific heat capacity'.

....

....

3 Assuming that two substances have an equal mass, will the substance with a higher or lower specific heat capacity have a greater temperature rise for the same input energy?

....

Calculations involving temperature changes in a system

4 In words, write the equation that links the change in thermal energy, change in temperature, mass and specific heat capacity.

....

5 Cooking oil has a specific heat capacity of 2000 J/kg°C.

How much energy would need to be supplied to 5 g of cooking oil to raise its temperature from 20°C to 100°C?

.... J

6 146.25 kJ of energy are supplied to 250 g of engine oil. The temperature of the oil rises from 20°C to 50°C.

Calculate the specific heat capacity of the engine oil in J/kg°C.

.... J/kg°C

7 101.5 kJ of energy are supplied to an aluminium saucepan. As a result, the temperature of the saucepan increases from 15°C to 220°C. The specific heat capacity of aluminium is 900 J/kg°C.

Calculate the mass of the saucepan in grams.

.... g

Changes of state and specific latent heat

Changes of state

The energy needed to cause a substance to change state is known as the **latent heat**. Latent heat is the energy that is added to a substance as it changes state; it is the energy needed to overcome the intermolecular forces.

The energy supplied during a state change increases the energy stored (the internal energy) but not the temperature.

Specific latent heat

The specific latent heat is the energy required to change the state of 1 kg of a substance without a change in temperature.

Just as different substances have different values for specific heat capacity, they also have different values for specific latent heat.

The **specific latent heat of fusion** is the energy required to melt 1 kg of a substance without a change in temperature.

The **specific latent heat of vaporisation** is the energy required to turn 1 kg of a liquid substance into a gas, without a change in temperature.

Calculations involving specific latent heat

The energy required to change the state of a substance depends on:
- the mass of the substance
- the specific latent heat of the substance.

The energy, mass and specific latent heat are related by the following equation:

$$E = mL$$

where

E is the energy supplied, in joules (J)

m is the mass of the substance, in kilograms (kg)

L is the specific latent heat of the substance, in joules per kilogram (J/kg)

Sometimes you will need to rearrange the equation $E = mL$ to make the unknown quantity the subject.

If the mass is unknown		If the specific latent heat is unknown	
$E = mL$ $m = \dfrac{E}{L}$	Divide both sides of the equation by L.	$E = mL$ $L = \dfrac{E}{m}$	Divide both sides of the equation by m.

The energy, mass and specific latent heat are linked by the equation $E = mL$

a) An ice cube has a mass of 7 g. The specific latent heat of fusion of water is 334 000 J/kg. Calculate the energy required to completely melt the ice cube.

List the information known about the ice cube.

Mass = $\frac{7}{1000}$ = 7 × 10⁻³ kg
Specific latent heat = 334 000 J/kg

Substitute these values into the equation for specific latent heat.

$E = mL = (7 \times 10^{-3}) \times 334\,000$
$E = 2338\,J$

b) A kettle has a capacity of 1.5 litres. When full, there is 1.5 kg of water in the kettle. Calculate the energy required to boil all of the water at 100°C in the kettle, given that the specific latent heat of vaporisation of water is 2 260 000 J/kg.

Begin by listing the information known about the water.

Mass = 1.5 kg
Specific latent heat = 2 260 000 J/kg

Substitute these values into the equation.

$E = mL = 1.5 \times 2\,260\,000$
$E = 3\,390\,000\,J = 3390\,kJ$

c) It takes 66 J of energy to melt a copper coin. The specific latent heat of fusion of copper is 13 200 J/kg. Calculate the coin's mass.

List the information known about the coin.

Energy = 66 J
Specific latent heat = 13 200 J/kg

Substitute these values into the equation.

$m = \dfrac{E}{L} = \dfrac{66}{13\,200}$
$m = 5 \times 10^{-3}$ kg

Changes of state and specific latent heat

Changes of state

1 Define the term 'latent heat'.

....

....

....

Specific latent heat

2 The specific latent heat of fusion and the specific latent heat of vaporisation can be used to calculate the energy required to change the state of a substance.

What is the difference between the specific latent heat of fusion and the specific latent heat of vaporisation?

....

....

....

Calculations involving specific latent heat

3 In words, write the equation that links energy, mass and specific latent heat.

....

4 Milk can be frozen to reduce wastage. Milk has a specific latent heat of fusion of 275 700 J/kg. Calculate the energy required to freeze 20 g of milk, assuming no change in temperature.

.... J

5 An aluminium block has a mass of 5 kg.

If 1995 kJ of energy are supplied in order to melt the block, calculate the specific latent heat of fusion of aluminium.

.... J/kg

6 1710 kJ of energy are needed to boil a sample of liquid lead. The specific latent heat of vaporisation of lead is 855 000 J/kg.

Calculate the mass of the lead sample.

.... kg

3 Particle motion in gases

The particle model

Anything that takes up space and mass is called **matter**. The particle model can be used to represent how matter is arranged and moves in each state of matter.

Solid

Liquid

Gas

Like all models, the particle model has limitations:
- particles are identical unless they are given different colours
- the individual atoms in the particles are not shown
- intermolecular forces between particles are not shown.

Particle motion in gases

The circles in the diagram represent the gas particles in a balloon.

The **direction** of the arrows represents the **direction** of movement of the particles and the **length** of the arrows represents the **speed** of the particles.

In conclusion, the particles in a gas:
- are in constant motion, with the speed and direction of the particles being random
- move at a range of speeds.

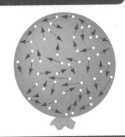

Motion, temperature and pressure in gases

The temperature of a gas is related to the **average kinetic energy** of all the gas particles in the substance. An increase in temperature leads to an increase in the average kinetic energy of the particles.

If the speed of the particles increases, so does the kinetic energy.

Changing the temperature of a gas, at constant volume, changes the pressure exerted by the gas. Pressure is caused by collisions between the gas particles and the walls of the container in which it is held.

If the temperature is increased, the average kinetic energy of the particles increases. This means that they will collide with the walls of the container **more frequently** and with **more energy**. The increasing frequency of collisions raises the pressure of the gas, since each collision creates a force.

Particles in a gas move in constant, random motion and at a range of speeds. As the temperature of a gas held at constant volume is increased, the pressure of the gas also increases.

You can calculate kinetic energy using the following equation:

$$E_k = \frac{1}{2}mv^2$$

where

E_k = kinetic energy, measured in joules (J)
m = mass, measured in kilograms (kg)
v = speed, measured in metres per second (m/s)

On average, the arrows are longer when the temperature is increased. This represents an increase in the speed of the particles.

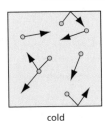

cold

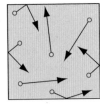

hot

③ Particle motion in gases

The particle model

1 State **two** limitations of the particle model of matter.

Solid

Liquid

Gas

....

....

Particle motion in gases

2 Describe the particle motion in gases. In your answer, refer to the direction and speed of the particles.

....

....

....

Motion, temperature and pressure in gases

3 Explain the effect of increasing the temperature of a gas on the average kinetic energy of the particles in the gas.

....

....

4 Using the equation for kinetic energy, explain the effect of doubling the kinetic energy on the average speed of the gas particles.

....

....

5 Explain what causes pressure when a gas is in a container.

....

....

6 Explain why, for a fixed mass of gas, an increase in temperature leads to an increase in pressure.

....

....

....

....

3 Pressure in gases

Pressure in gases

The **volume** of a gas can be increased or decreased by altering the pressure of the gas.

For a gas at constant temperature and mass, **the larger the volume, the lower the pressure**. This is because the larger volume increases the area over which collisions can occur with the walls of the container. This reduces the net force caused by the gas particles on the walls, in turn reducing the pressure exerted by the gas.

Low pressure   High pressure

At low pressure, the gas particles are far apart. In contrast, at high pressure, the particles are forced closer together.

Calculating pressure in gases

For a fixed mass of gas held at a constant temperature:

$$pV = \text{constant}$$

where

p is the pressure, in pascals (Pa)

V is the volume, in cubic metres (m^3)

This relationship allows you to calculate the final pressure if the volume of the gas is changed.

$$p_1V_1 = p_2V_2$$

where

p_1 is the initial pressure p_2 is the final pressure

V_1 is the initial volume V_2 is the final volume

a) A balloon is filled with 0.1 m^3 of gas at atmospheric pressure (100 000 Pa). The volume of the balloon is reduced to 0.05 m^3. Calculate the final pressure of the gas in the balloon.

Begin by listing the information known about the gas

$p_1 = 100\,000\,Pa$

$V_1 = 0.1\,m^3$

$V_2 = 0.05\,m^3$

Substitute these values into the equation for gas pressure

$p_1V_1 = p_2V_2$

$100\,000 \times 0.1 = p_2 \times 0.05$

Divide both sides of the equation by 0.05 to calculate the final pressure, p_2

$p_2 = \frac{(100\,000 \times 0.1)}{0.05}$

$p_2 = 200\,000\,Pa$

b) 0.01 m^3 of gas is in a syringe at a pressure of 100 000 Pa. The pressure in the syringe is reduced to 25 000 Pa. Calculate the new volume of the gas.

List the information known about the gas

$p_1 = 100\,000\,Pa$

$V_1 = 0.01\,m^3$

$p_2 = 25\,000\,Pa$

Substitute these values into the equation for gas pressure

$p_1V_1 = p_2V_2$

$100\,000 \times 0.01 = 25\,000 \times V_2$

Divide both sides of the equation by 25 000 to calculate the final volume, V_2

$V_2 = \frac{(100\,000 \times 0.1)}{25\,000}$

$V_2 = 0.04\,m^3$

For a fixed mass of gas held at a constant temperature, pressure × volume = constant, so $p_1V_1 = p_2V_2$

Pressure in gases

Pressure in gases

1 Use the particle model to explain why an increase in volume at a constant temperature leads to a decrease in pressure of a gas.

....

....

....

Calculating pressure in gases

2 Complete the sentence below.

If the pressure of a fixed mass of gas at constant temperature is halved, the volume of the gas

....

3 A sample of air at a pressure of 100 kPa occupies a volume of 25 cm³.

Calculate the pressure of the gas if its volume is doubled.

.... Pa

4 A gas canister of volume 1 dm³ contains gas at a pressure of 25 000 Pa.

Calculate the volume of the gas if it is allowed to reach atmospheric pressure (100 000 Pa). Give your answer in cm³.

.... cm³

5 A sample of gas occupies a volume of 10 m³. If the volume of the gas is increased to 20 m³, the pressure of the gas is 10 000 Pa.

Calculate the initial pressure of the gas.

.... Pa

6 A sample of gas at a pressure of 2.5×10^7 Pa is compressed to a new volume of 0.3 m³. This increases the pressure of the gas to 5.5×10^7 Pa.

Calculate the initial volume of the gas in m³.

.... m³

Structure of the atom, mass and atomic number, and isotopes

Structure of the atom

An atom is the smallest particle of an element that can exist. Atoms are tiny, with diameters of about 1×10^{-10} m.

An atom has **protons**, **neutrons** and **electrons**. All atoms of a particular element have the same number of protons.

Atomic particle	Relative mass	Relative charge
Proton	1	+1
Neutron	1	0
Electron	0 (nearly)	−1

An atom has the same number of protons as electrons. So, an atom as a whole has no electrical charge.

The electrons are located in energy levels at varying distances from the nucleus.

The nucleus of an atom contains the protons and neutrons. The radius of the nucleus is about 10 000 smaller than the radius of the atom.

The diameter of a gold nucleus is 3×10^{-14} m. The diameter of a sodium nucleus is 3×10^{-15} m. How many times larger is the gold nucleus than the sodium nucleus?

Ratio $= \frac{3 \times 10^{-14}}{3 \times 10^{-15}} = 10$

So, the gold nucleus is 10 times larger than the sodium nucleus.

> Calculate the ratio of the diameters of the nuclei to compare one to the other.

The electron configuration can be altered by the absorption or emission of electromagnetic radiation:

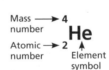

- If electromagnetic radiation is absorbed by the atom, an electron may move to a higher energy level further away from the nucleus.
- If electromagnetic radiation is emitted, an electron falls down to a lower energy level.

Mass and atomic number

Atoms of different elements have different numbers of protons.

The number of protons defines the element:
- The number of protons in an atom is called its **atomic number**.
- The number of protons and neutrons in an atom is called its **mass number**.

Mass number → 4
Atomic number → 2 He ← Element symbol

To calculate the number of...	protons	electrons	neutrons
Use...	the atomic number	the atomic number	the mass number – the atomic number

Calculate the number of neutrons in a sodium nucleus. $^{23}_{11}$Na

> To calculate the number of neutrons, subtract the atomic number from the mass number.

The mass number is 23 and the atomic number is 11.

The number of neutrons $= 23 - 11 = 12$

Isotopes

Some atoms of the same element can have different numbers of neutrons. These are called **isotopes**.

> Atoms have a nucleus that contains protons and neutrons, surrounded by electrons in energy levels. Isotopes are atoms of the same element with the same number of protons, but a different number of neutrons.

Calculate the number of neutrons in each of the three isotopes of carbon: $^{12}_{6}$C $^{13}_{6}$C $^{14}_{6}$C

> Subtract the atomic number from the mass number for each isotope.

Carbon-12: No. of neutrons $= 12 - 6 = 6$
Carbon-13: No. of neutrons $= 13 - 6 = 7$
Carbon-14: No. of neutrons $= 14 - 6 = 8$

Structure of the atom, mass and atomic number, and isotopes

Structure of the atom

1 Complete this table showing the relative masses and charges of the three subatomic particles.

Atomic particle	Relative mass	Relative charge
Proton		
Neutron		
Electron		

2 The diameter of a uranium nucleus is 1.5×10^{-14} m.
The diameter of a sodium nucleus is 1.7×10^{-15} m.

How many times bigger is a uranium nucleus than a helium nucleus?

Mass and atomic number

3 Find the number of neutrons in an aluminium nucleus, given this information:

$$^{27}_{13}\text{Al}$$

4 What can be deduced about a magnesium atom from this information?

$$^{24}_{12}\text{Mg}$$

Number of: protons = ...   electrons = ...   neutrons = ...

Isotopes

5 What is meant by the term 'isotope'?

6 Give **one similarity** and **one difference** in structure of these isotopes of hydrogen.

$$^{1}_{1}\text{H}$$

hydrogen-1 (protium)

$$^{2}_{1}\text{H}$$

hydrogen-2 (deuterium)

$$^{3}_{1}\text{H}$$

hydrogen-3 (tritium)

Similarity: ....

Difference: ....

(4) Development of the model of the atom

The solid sphere model

Theories about what matter consists of have been developing since the time of Greek philosopher Democritus (circa 460–370 BCE).

Prior to the discovery of the electron, atoms were thought to be tiny, solid spheres that could not be divided further. The term **atom** comes from the Greek adjective, *atomos*, which means **indivisible**.

The plum pudding model

In 1897, JJ Thomson discovered the **electron**. The discovery of the electron led to the model of the atom being revised.

He proposed that atoms consisted of a positively charged sphere, in which negatively charged electrons were scattered.

This model became known as the '**plum pudding model**' as it was thought that the electrons represented plums embedded into a sponge pudding.

The nuclear model

In 1911, Ernest Rutherford carried out some experiments in which alpha particles were directed at a thin film of gold foil.

This led to the suggestion that:

- most of the atom was empty space, as most alpha particles passed straight through the foil
- the centre of the atom contained a positively charged nucleus, as some of the positively charged alpha particles were deflected
- the nucleus was extremely tiny, and that this was where all the mass and charge of the atom was contained.

This became known as the **nuclear model** of the atom.

Atoms

A very small number of alpha particles deflected straight back

Most alpha particles passed straight through

Some alpha particles deflected through at small angles

New experimental evidence can lead to a scientific model being changed or replaced.

The Bohr model

In 1913, Niels Bohr adapted the nuclear model of the atom to put electrons orbiting at specific distances from the nucleus. His calculations agreed with experimental observations at the time and so the model of the atom was again revised.

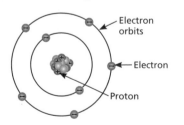

Electron orbits

Electron

Proton

Discovery of the neutron

In 1932, nearly 20 years after the nucleus became an accepted scientific idea, James Chadwick discovered the **neutron**. This led to the current model of the atom, which includes neutrons in the nucleus of an atom.

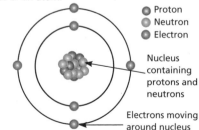

Proton
Neutron
Electron

Nucleus containing protons and neutrons

Electrons moving around nucleus

Development of the model of the atom

The solid sphere model

1. Describe the solid sphere model of the atom.

The plum pudding model

2. The discovery of which particle led to the plum pudding model being suggested? ....

3. Draw a diagram to represent the plum pudding model of the atom.

The nuclear model

4. Draw a line from each experimental observation on the left to the corresponding conclusion about the structure of the atom made from the alpha scattering experiment.

Experimental observation	Conclusion
Most alpha particles passed straight through the gold foil	The nucleus is very small and very dense
Some alpha particles were deflected at small angles	Most of the atom is empty space
A very small number of alpha particles were deflected straight back	The nucleus is positively charged

The Bohr model

5. Draw a diagram to represent the Bohr model of the atom. Show the electrons and protons.

Discovery of the neutron

6. Who discovered the neutron in 1932? ....

(4) Radioactive decay and nuclear radiation

Radioactive decay

Radioactive isotopes (radioisotopes or radionuclides) are atoms with unstable nuclei. They may disintegrate and emit **radiation**. This is **radioactive decay**.

Radioactive decay can result in the formation of a different atom with a different number of protons.

Two examples of radioactive decay are alpha (α) radiation and beta (β) radiation. A third type is gamma (γ) radiation. However, unlike alpha and beta, gamma emissions have no effect on the structure of the nucleus.

Radioactive decay is a **random** process: it is impossible to tell **which** nuclei will decay or **when** a particular nucleus will decay.

> There are three types of nuclear radiation: alpha decay, beta decay and gamma emission.

Alpha (α) decay	Beta (β) decay
In alpha decay, the original atom decays by ejecting an alpha particle from the nucleus.	In beta decay, the original atom decays by changing a neutron into a proton and an electron.
An alpha particle is a helium nucleus – a particle made up of two protons and two neutrons.	The newly formed high-energy electron ejected from the nucleus is a β particle.
A new atom is formed with α decay.	A new atom is formed with β decay.

| Unstable nucleus | New nucleus | α particle | | Unstable nucleus | New nucleus | β particle |

Ionisation

Radioactive particles can collide with neutral atoms or molecules. Electrons will be knocked out of their structure and they will become charged. These charged particles are called **ions**.

Alpha radiation and beta radiation are known as **ionising radiation**.

Ionising radiation can damage molecules in a healthy cell, causing the death of the cell.

Activity and count rate

The rate at which a source of unstable nuclei decay is known as the **activity** of the source. The **activity** is measured in **becquerels** (Bq).

The **count rate** is the number of decays per second that are recorded by a detector, such as a Geiger-Muller tube. Count rate is also measured in **becquerels**.

Source Am-241   G-M tube   Ratemeter

Properties of alpha, beta and gamma radiation

Type of radiation	Alpha	Beta	Gamma
Penetration power	Stopped by skin or a single sheet of paper	Stopped by 2–3 mm of aluminium foil	Stopped by thick lead or concrete
Range in air	< 5 cm	~ 1 m	> 1 km
Ionising power	High	Low	Very low

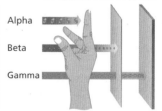

Alpha

Beta

Gamma

Skin Aluminium Lead

Radioactive decay and nuclear radiation

Radioactive decay

1 What is meant by the term 'radioactive decay'?

2 What is meant by the 'random nature' of radioactive decay?

3 What does an alpha particle consist of?

4 Explain why a new element is formed in the process of alpha decay.

5 In beta decay, a neutron decays inside an unstable nucleus.

Into which **two** particles does the neutron decay?

Ionisation

6 What effect can ionisation have on healthy cells in the body?

Activity and count rate

7 What is the difference between the 'activity' and the 'count rate' of a source?

Properties of alpha, beta and gamma radiation

8 Complete the table to compare the properties of alpha, beta and gamma radiation.

Type of radiation	Penetration power	Range in air	Ionising power
Alpha	Stopped by	< 5 cm	
Beta	Stopped by 2–3 mm of aluminium foil		Low
Gamma	Stopped by		

4 Nuclear equations

What are nuclear equations?

Nuclear equations can be used to represent radioactive decay.

Loss of an alpha or a beta particle from the nucleus may result in a change in the mass of the nucleus and/or a change in the charge of the nucleus.

Gamma radiation is the emission of a high energy, high frequency electromagnetic wave which is uncharged and has no mass. Therefore, emission of a gamma wave from a nucleus does not cause the mass or the charge to change.

An alpha particle is represented by the symbol

$$^{4}_{2}\text{He}$$

A beta particle is represented by the symbol

$$^{0}_{-1}\text{e}$$

Remember that a beta particle is a fast-moving electron.

Nuclear equations to represent alpha and beta decay

Nuclear equations can be used to represent both alpha and beta decay.

A represents the mass number; Z represents the atomic number.

Alpha decay	Beta decay
The mass number of radon is 219. The atomic mass of polonium is 215. Alpha decay causes the **mass number to decrease by 4**.	The mass number of carbon is 14. The atomic mass of nitrogen is also 14. Beta decay causes the **mass number to remain unchanged**.

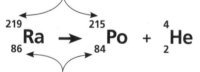

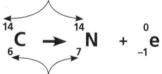

The atomic number for radon is 86, whereas the atomic number for the resultant nucleus, polonium, is 84. So alpha decay causes the **atomic number to decrease by 2**.

$$^{A}_{Z}X \rightarrow ^{A-4}_{Z-2}Y + ^{4}_{2}\text{He}$$

The atomic number for carbon is 6 and the atomic number for the resultant nucleus, nitrogen, is 7. So beta decay causes the **atomic number to increase by 1**.

$$^{A}_{Z}X \rightarrow ^{A}_{Z+1}Y + ^{0}_{-1}\text{e}$$

Balancing nuclear equations

Complete the nuclear equation for the decay of uranium-238 into thorium-234 by alpha decay adding the missing values, X and Y, into the equation shown.

$$^{238}_{92}U \rightarrow ^{234}_{Y}\text{Th} + ^{X}_{2}\text{He}$$

Begin by considering the atomic masses of the particles.

The atomic masses have to balance:
$238 = 234 + X$
$X = 238 - 234$
$X = 4$

Then consider the atomic numbers of the particles.

The atomic numbers have to balance, so:
$92 = Y + 2$
$Y = 92 - 2$
$Y = 90$

In nuclear equations, the atomic masses and atomic numbers must balance on either side of the arrow.

4 Nuclear equations

What are nuclear equations?

1 Write the symbols used to represent:

a) an alpha particle ....

b) a beta particle ....

2 Explain why the emission of a gamma wave from a radioactive nucleus **does not** result in a change in mass or charge of the nucleus.

....

....

....

Nuclear equations to represent alpha and beta decay

3 Complete the table to show the effect of alpha decay on the values for atomic number and atomic mass number.

	Atomic number	Atomic mass number
After alpha decay	Decreases by	.... by 4

4 Complete the table to show the effect of beta decay on the values for atomic number and atomic mass number.

	Atomic number	Atomic mass number
After beta decay	Increases by	

Balancing nuclear equations

5 Calculate the values for X and Y in the nuclear equation below.

$$^{239}_{Y}\text{Pu} \rightarrow {}^{X}_{92}\text{U} + {}^{4}_{2}\text{He}$$

$X = $ ....

$Y = $ ....

6 Balance the nuclear equation below.

$$^{}_{6}\text{C} \rightarrow {}^{11}_{}\text{B} + {}^{}_{-1}\text{e}$$

Half-lives and the random nature of radioactive decay

Half-life

The decay of a radioactive isotope is **random**, meaning that it is not possible to tell:
- when a particular nucleus will decay
- which nuclei will decay at any given time.

Despite the random nature, all radioactive isotope decays follow a similar pattern. If a sample contains 1000 nuclei, then after a certain amount of time 500 will remain. Once the same amount of time has passed again, 250 nuclei will remain.

The time taken for the number of nuclei of an isotope in a sample to halve is the **half-life**.

Different radioactive isotopes have different half-lives, ranging from less than 1 second to more than 1000 years.

An alternative way to define half-life is the time it takes for the count rate (or activity) of the sample to fall to half of its initial value.

> The half-life of a sample is the time taken for half of the nuclei in a sample to decay, or the time taken for the activity of the sample to fall to half of its original value.

Using graphs to determine half-life

It is possible to determine the half-life of a radioisotope using a graph:

1. Locate the point on the y-axis where the value has fallen to half the original value $\left(\frac{A_0}{2}\right)$.
2. Draw a horizontal straight line from this value to meet the curve.
3. Draw a vertical straight line down from the point where it meets the curve to the value on the x-axis. This gives you the first half-life, $t_{\frac{1}{2}}$.
4. Repeat, finding where the value on the y-axis falls by half again (so a quarter of its original value, $\frac{A_0}{4}$).

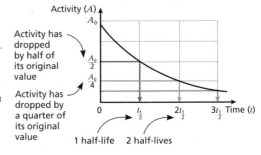

5. The time from the first half-life to this one is the second half-life.
6. Repeat for a third time and take an average of the half-lives.

Using half-lives

a) A radioactive isotope has a half-life of 12 minutes. Assuming that there were 100 nuclei in the sample at the start, how many nuclei remain after 60 minutes?

Time (minutes)	Number of nuclei remaining
0	100
12 (after 1 half-life)	50
24 (after 2 half-lives)	25
36 (after 3 half-lives)	12
48 (after 4 half-lives)	6
60 (after 5 half-lives)	3

After 60 minutes, 3 nuclei remain.

b) The half-life of carbon-14 is 5700 years. If there are 10 g of carbon-14 in a sample, how much will remain after 22 800 years?

Begin by calculating the number of half-lives that have passed.

$\frac{22\,800}{5700} = 4$ half-lives

Now calculate the proportion of the sample that will remain after 4 half-lives.

$\left(\frac{1}{2}\right)^4 = \frac{1}{16}$

So, $\frac{1}{16}$ th of the sample will remain.

Finally, calculate what $\frac{1}{16}$ th of 10 g is.

$\frac{1}{16} \times 10 = 0.625$ g will remain after 22 800 years.

RETRIEVE 4 — Half-lives and the random nature of radioactive decay

Half-life

1 What is meant by the 'random nature' of radioactive decay?

....

....

2 What is the 'half-life' of a radioisotope?

....

....

Using graphs to determine half-life

3 Determine the half-life of this isotope.

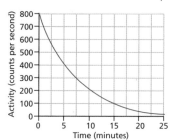

.... minutes

Using half-lives

4 Cobalt-60 has a half-life of 5 days.

Assuming that a sample has an initial activity of 600 Bq, what will be the activity of the sample after 30 days? Use a table (on a separate piece of paper) in your answer.

.... Bq

5 Caesium-137 has a half-life of 30 years.

a) What proportion of a 1 kg sample will remain after 120 years?

....

b) How much of the sample will remain after 120 years?

.... g

Radioactive contamination

What is meant by irradiation and contamination?

Irradiation		Contamination	
If an object is **irradiated**, it has been exposed to nuclear radiation: • the irradiated object does **not** become radioactive • the irradiation stops as soon as the source is removed.	Object exposed to radiation	If an object is **contaminated**, there is a presence of material containing radioactive atoms on or in the object: • the contaminated object remains radioactive for as long as the source is on/in it • the hazard from contamination is due to the decay of the contaminating atoms.	Radiation placed in or on object

Irradiation

If an object is irradiated, living cells can be damaged. This can be both problematic and beneficial.

Sterilisation	Medical treatment
 Gamma rays → Bacteria killed Fruit can be exposed to cobalt-60, which emits gamma rays. These gamma rays can kill bacteria on the surface of the fruit, preserving it and extending its shelf-life. In a similar way, irradiation is also used to sterilise surgical instruments.	Gamma rays can be directed towards the site of tumours to kill cancerous tissue. Care must be taken to calculate the correct dose as local healthy tissues can also be damaged in the process.  Gamma rays Protective head gear Cancerous tumour

Contamination

Contamination of an object can cause problems, but is useful in other ways.

Checking for leaks in underground pipes	Medical contamination
It is easy to see a leak in a water pipe above ground, but not if it is underground. If a leak is suspected, a gamma-emitting isotope can be introduced into the water supply. If water gathers at the site of a leak, the build-up of the gamma ray emission can be detected. This helps to identify the source of the leak.	Tracers, such as technicium-99, can be used for medical purposes. Medical tracers show up soft tissue as the gamma rays that are emitted by the tracer can pass through the body and be detected. If there is a blockage in a blood vessel, for example, the tracer will stop flowing through the body and build up at the site. This can then be investigated by camera.

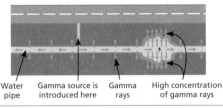

Water pipe — Gamma source is introduced here — Gamma rays — High concentration of gamma rays

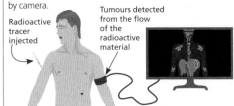

Radioactive tracer injected — Tumours detected from the flow of the radioactive material

The process of contaminating substances needs careful consideration as it can be difficult to remove all the contaminating material once it is no longer needed. It is important to consider the half-life of the substances used: it should give enough time without causing long-standing contamination.

> Contamination and irradiation can be both useful and problematic.

4 Radioactive contamination

What is meant by irradiation and contamination?

1 Give **one similarity** and **one difference** between irradiation and contamination.

Similarity: ....

....

....

Difference: ....

....

....

Irradiation

2 How is irradiation used to extend the shelf-life of some foods, such as apples?

....

....

....

3 Give **one** medical use for irradiation.

....

Contamination

4 There is a suspected gas leak in an underground pipe.

Explain how radioactive contamination of the gas supply could help to identify the source of the leak.

....

....

....

....

....

5 Suggest what measures should be taken to ensure that radioactive contamination of the gas supply in question 4 does **not** cause unnecessary harm to residents.

....

....

....

....

....

Hazards and uses of radioactive emissions and background radiation

Background radiation

Background radiation is around us all of the time.

Sources of background radiation

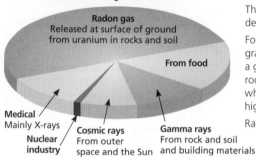

Radon gas
Released at surface of ground from uranium in rocks and soil

From food

Medical
Mainly X-rays

Nuclear
industry

Cosmic rays
From outer
space and the Sun

Gamma rays
From rock and soil
and building materials

Notice that the vast majority of background radiation comes from natural sources.

The level of background radiation exposure can depend on both occupation and location.

For example, Cornwall has a large amount of granite in the ground, so people living there have a greater exposure to background radiation from rocks than residents in other locations. People who work in hospitals are likely to be exposed to a higher level of background radiation from X-rays.

Radiation dose is measured in **sieverts** (**Sv**).

Different half-lives of radioisotopes

When evaluating the uses of a radioisotope, it is important to consider its half-life.

The fuel used in nuclear power stations has a very long half-life (in the region of millions of years). This means that, in the event of a nuclear accident, radioactive material will be present for millions of years. For this reason, great care needs to be taken in the disposal of nuclear waste as a higher quantity increases its activity.

Beta and gamma sources, such as technitium-99 (known as 9943Tc), are used as medical tracers. The half-life of 9943Tc is 6.05 hours. This means that the radioisotope is active for long enough for the scan to take place but it soon decays to very low levels.

Uses of nuclear radiation

Nuclear radiation is used in medicine as both a diagnostic aid and as a treatment. Medical tracers are used to locate areas of concern, such as blockages or tumours.

The radioisotope is ingested into the body and then followed, using a camera. For this reason, beta or gamma sources are used; alpha particles would not pass through the body and so would be undetectable. In addition, alpha particles are highly ionising and would be very dangerous inside the body as they would damage or kill healthy cells.

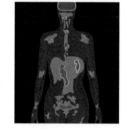

Gamma radioisotopes are used to destroy tumours.

Lots of gamma rays are directed towards the tumour as, individually, they are not strong enough to destroy the tumour. This means that healthy cells around the tumour receive a lower dose of the gamma radiation.

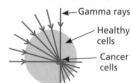

Gamma rays

Healthy cells

Cancer cells

It is important to limit the exposure of the healthy cells to the gamma radiation, so this type of treatment is used sparingly where the benefits are deemed to outweigh the risks of exposing healthy cells to gamma radiation.

> Different radioisotopes have very different half-lives and this needs to be considered when deciding which one to use. They are used for both medical diagnosis and treatment.

RETRIEVE 4 — Hazards and uses of radioactive emissions and background radiation

Background radiation

1 Name **three** natural sources of background radiation.

_____

_____

_____

2 State the unit used to measure radiation dose.

_____

Different half-lives of radioisotopes

3 The fuel used in nuclear reactors has a very long half-life.

Explain why great care needs to be taken in the disposal of nuclear waste.

_____

_____

_____

_____

_____

Uses of nuclear radiation

4 Explain why radioisotopes used as medical tracers need to be either beta or gamma sources rather than alpha sources.

_____

_____

_____

_____

5 Give **one advantage** and **one disadvantage** of using gamma radiation to destroy cancerous tumours.

Advantage: _____

_____

Disadvantage: _____

_____

Nuclear fission and fusion

Nuclear fission

Nuclear fission is the splitting of atomic nuclei. It is used in nuclear reactors to produce energy to make electricity. Uranium-235 and plutonium-239 are often used.

The products of nuclear fission are radioactive so there is a danger of reactions potentially getting out of control (e.g. the Chernobyl disaster of 1986). However, the benefit for power generation is the large amount of energy that is released by an atom during nuclear fission.

> Nuclear fission is the process of splitting of atomic nuclei. It is used in nuclear reactors to produce energy to make electricity.

Nuclear fission on a small scale

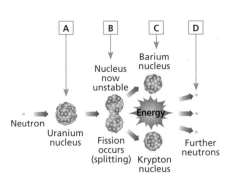

Nuclear fission on a large scale

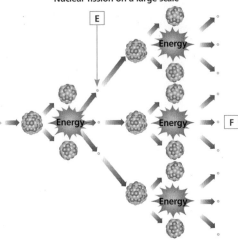

A | The uranium atom absorbs a neutron that collides with its nucleus.

B | The nucleus splits up into two smaller nuclei (e.g. barium and krypton).

C | This releases energy and new neutrons.

D | The new atoms formed (barium and krypton) are themselves radioactive.

E | The new neutrons produced by nuclear fission can each cause a new fission. This is a **chain reaction**. It carries on and on and on.

F | The energy is released in the form of heat. Each fission reaction only produces a tiny amount of energy, but there are billions and billions of reactions every second.

Nuclear fusion

Nuclear fusion is the joining together of two or more atomic nuclei to form a larger atomic nucleus. A lot of energy is needed for the nuclei to fuse.

A nuclear fusion reaction generally releases more energy than it uses. This makes it self-sustaining, i.e. some of the energy produced is used to drive further fusion reactions.

Stars release energy by nuclear fusion. In the core of the Sun, hydrogen is converted to helium by fusion. This provides the energy to keep the Sun burning and allow life on Earth.

> Nuclear fusion is the process of the joining together of two or more atomic nuclei to form a larger atomic nucleus.

An example is the fusion of two heavy forms of hydrogen (deuterium and tritium). When they are forced together, the deuterium and tritium nuclei fuse to form a new helium atom and an unchanged neutron.

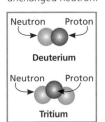

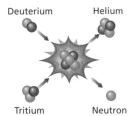

Nuclear fission and fusion

Nuclear fission

1. Name the **two** most common fuels used in nuclear fission reactors.

   ....

2. Name the particle absorbed by a uranium or plutonium nucleus to start a nuclear fission reaction.

   ....

3. Name the **three** products of a fission reaction.

   ....

   ....

   ....

4. Complete the right-hand side of this diagram to show a nuclear fission chain reaction.

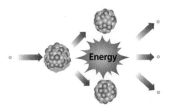

Nuclear fusion

5. What is meant by 'nuclear fusion'?

   ....

   ....

6. Describe the process of nuclear fusion in the Sun.

   ....

   ....

   ....

(5) Physical quantities

Scalar and vector quantities

Physics is concerned with taking measurements of the world around us. Physical quantities are those that can be measured.

There are two types of physical quantity: **scalar** and **vector** quantities.

Scalar quantities have **magnitude** (or size) only.

Energy

Mass

Time

Examples of scalar quantities

Temperature

Speed

Vector quantities have **magnitude** (or size) and **direction**.

Force

Displacement

Velocity

Examples of vector quantities

Acceleration

Momentum

Vector quantities are often represented using arrows:

- The length of the arrow represents the magnitude of the quantity.
- The direction of the arrow represents the direction of the quantity.

> Scalar quantities have magnitude only. Vector quantities have magnitude and direction.

For example, a force of 10 N to the left could be represented as an arrow like this:

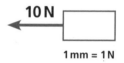

10 N

1 mm = 1 N

Notice the use of a scale in the diagram. This allows large magnitudes to be represented.

Contact and non-contact forces

Force is an example of a **vector** quantity, as forces can act in different directions.

Contact forces occur when two objects are physically in contact with one another.

Examples of contact forces include:

- friction, e.g. between the tyres of a bicycle and the road surface, which will cause the tyres to become warm
- air resistance, e.g. a parachutist falling through the air, which will slow the parachutist down
- normal contact force, e.g. a pencil case resting on the table
- tension, e.g. a string holding up a child's cot mobile, preventing it from falling.

> Contact forces occur when two objects are physically in contact with one another, whereas non-contact forces occur without them being physically in contact.

Non-contact forces occur without two objects being physically in contact with one another.

Examples of non-contact forces include:

- gravitational force, which causes masses to be attracted to one another, e.g. the Earth is attracted to the Sun by a gravitational force
- electrostatic force; this exists between charged objects
- magnetic force; this is experienced by any magnetic object when placed in a magnetic field, e.g. opposite poles of a magnet are attracted to one another; like poles repel one another.

(5) Physical quantities

Scalar and vector quantities

1 What is meant by a 'scalar' quantity?

....

2 Give **two** examples of scalar quantities.

....

....

3 What is the difference between a scalar and a vector quantity?

....

....

4 Give **two** examples of vector quantities.

....

....

5 Draw a diagram to represent a force on a box of 40 N to the left and 70 N to the right.

What is the resultant force acting on the object?

.... N to the ....

Contact and non-contact forces

6 Give **three** examples of contact forces.

....

....

....

7 Give **three** examples of non-contact forces.

....

....

....

5 Gravity

What is gravity?

The Earth's gravitational field is the region around the Earth, where objects experience its force of gravity.

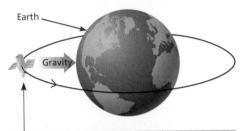

Orbiting satellite experiences an attractive gravitational force towards the Earth. The force of gravity stops it from flying off into outer space.

The Earth's gravitational field strength is defined as the gravitational force on a mass of 1 kg. It is given the symbol *g* and is measured in units of newtons per kilogram (N/kg).

The Earth's gravitational field exerts a force on an apple in a tree. If the apple's stem breaks, the force of gravity causes it to fall faster and faster (until terminal velocity is reached) from the tree to the ground.

When the apple is on the ground, the Earth is still exerting a downward force of gravity on it. However, the apple does not continue to fall because an upward contact force is exerted on it by the ground.

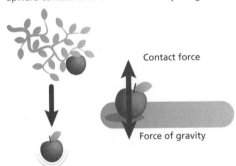

Contact force

Force of gravity

Weight

The force of gravity on an object is also known as its **weight**. The weight of an object can be thought of acting at a single point: the object's 'centre of mass'.

Weight, mass and gravitational field strength are linked by the following equation:

$$W = mg$$
where

W is the weight, in newtons (N)

m is the mass, in kilograms (kg)

g is the gravitational field strength, in newtons per kilogram (N/kg)

At the Earth's surface, the value of g is about 10 N/kg. This means that a mass of 1 kg experiences a force of gravity of 10 N.

The mass of the satellite in the diagram above is 1200 kg. Work out its weight on Earth, given that the gravitational field strength on Earth is 10 N/kg.

$W = mg$

$\quad = 1200 \times 10$

$\quad = 12\,000$ N

Sometimes the mass or the gravitational field strength will not be known, so you will need to rearrange the equation to make the unknown quantity the subject.

If the mass is unknown	If the gravitational field strength is unknown
$W = mg$ $\dfrac{W}{g} = m$ Divide both sides of the equation by g.	$W = mg$ $\dfrac{W}{m} = g$ Divide both sides of the equation by m.

Weight is the force of gravity on an object and can be calculated using the equation $W = mg$

5 Gravity

What is gravity?

1 What is meant by the 'gravitational field strength'? State the units in which it is measured.

2 Draw a diagram to show the direction of the force of gravity on a satellite orbiting the Earth.

Weight

3 Define the term 'weight'. State the units in which it is measured.

4 In words, write the equation that links gravitational field strength, mass and weight.

5 A box has a mass of 5 kg.

Calculate the weight of the box, given that the gravitational field strength on Earth is 10 N/kg.

.... N

6 An astronaut has a mass of 65 kg. On the Moon, the weight of the astronaut is 104 N.

Calculate the gravitational field strength on the Moon.

.... N/kg

⑤ Resultant forces

What are resultant forces?

The movement of an object depends on the forces acting on it. If the forces are equal and opposite, they are balanced and so the resultant force is zero.

If the forces are not equal and opposite, they are unbalanced and the resultant force is not zero.

If the resultant force acting on a **stationary** object is:
- zero, the object will remain stationary

200 N push   Friction 200 N

- not zero, the object will start to move in the direction of the resultant force.

400 N push   Friction 200 N

If the resultant force acting on a **moving** object is:
- zero, the object will continue at the same speed in the same direction

200 N push   Friction 200 N

- not zero, the object will speed up or slow down in the direction of the resultant force.

0 N push   Friction 200 N

> Forces acting on an object can be added or subtracted to give a resultant force.

Free body diagrams

Free body diagrams show the direction and magnitude of all forces acting on an object. The object is shown as a box or a dot.

The free body diagram shows the forces acting on an aeroplane. The length of the arrows is drawn to scale: the longer the arrow, the greater the force. In this example, the weight and the upthrust are equal and the thrust is greater than the air resistance. This means that the aeroplane will move to the right.

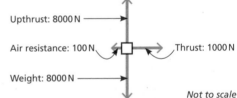
Upthrust: 8000 N
Air resistance: 100 N   Thrust: 1000 N
Weight: 8000 N
Not to scale

⊞ Resolving forces

Sometimes it is useful to **resolve** a single force into its two components: the **horizontal** component and the **vertical** component.

A person pulls on a sled with a force of 100 N at an angle of 40° to the horizontal:

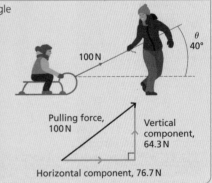
100 N
θ 40°

In order to resolve the force of 100 N into the horizontal and vertical components, follow these steps:
1. Draw an arrow representing the 100 N force at 40° to the horizontal. Using a scale 1 cm : 10 N, this arrow would be 10 cm long.
2. Draw a horizontal line that ends directly below the 100 N arrow.
3. Draw a vertical line joining the ends of the horizontal line and the 100 N arrow.
4. Add arrowheads to the horizontal and vertical lines.
5. Measure the length of the horizontal and vertical lines.
6. Apply the scale used to draw the original arrow to determine the magnitude of the horizontal and vertical components.

Pulling force, 100 N
Vertical component, 64.3 N
Horizontal component, 76.7 N

⑤ Resultant forces

What are resultant forces?

1 Calculate the resultant force acting on the box in the diagram.

5 N 10 N

Resultant force = _____ N _____

2 Calculate the resultant force acting on the ball in the diagram.

5 N

7 N

Resultant force = _____ N _____

Free body diagrams

3 Draw a free body diagram to show the forces acting on the boat in the diagram. Label the forces on your diagram.

4 Draw a free body diagram to represent the forces acting on the books in the diagram. Label the forces on your diagram.

HT Resolving forces

5 A person walking a dog pulls with a force of 50 N on the lead, at an angle of 37° to the horizontal.

Using a scale diagram, on a separate piece of paper, determine the horizontal and vertical components of this force.

Horizontal component = _____ N

Vertical component = _____ N

Work done and energy transfer

Work done

When a force moves an object, **work** is done on the object resulting in the **transfer** of **energy**.

In the image, the woman is pushing the wheelbarrow, causing it to move. There is a transfer of energy from the chemical store of the woman to the kinetic store of the wheelbarrow. You can say that **work** has been done on the wheelbarrow.

The work done is equal to the energy transferred. Energy is measured in joules (J), so work done is also measured in joules (J).

> work done (J) = energy transferred (J)

Calculating work done

You can calculate the work done on an object using the following equation:

$$W = Fs$$

where

W is the work done, in joules (J)

F is the force, in newtons (N)

s is the distance, in metres (m)

1 joule of work is equal to a force of 1 newton causing a displacement of 1 metre, so $1\,J = 1\,Nm$.

Sometimes the force or the distance of the object will not be known, so you will need to rearrange the equation $W = Fs$ to make the unknown quantity the subject. Remember that when rearranging equations, whatever is done to one side must be done to the other.

If the force is unknown	$W = Fs$ $\dfrac{W}{s} = F$	Divide both sides of the equation by distance.
If the distance is unknown	$W = Fs$ $\dfrac{W}{F} = s$	Divide both sides of the equation by force.

Work done against frictional forces is mainly transformed into heat energy. When work is done on an elastic object to change its shape, the energy is stored in the object as elastic potential energy.

> Work done = force × distance, so $1\,J = 1\,Nm$

a) A football is kicked with a force of 10 N. It travels a distance of 15 m.

Calculate the work done on the football as it is kicked.

Begin by listing the information known about the football.

Force = 10 N
Distance = 15 m

Substitute these values into the equation for work done.

$W = Fs$
$W = 10 \times 15$
$W = 150\,J$

b) A man pushes a car with a steady force of 250 N. The car moves a distance of 20 m. How much work does the man do?

Substitute these values into the equation for work done.

$W = Fs$
$W = 250 \times 20$
$W = 5000\,J$ (or 5 kJ)

Work done and energy transfer

Work done

1 What is meant by the term 'work done'?

....

2 In words, write down the relationship between work done and energy transferred.

....

Calculating work done

3 In words, write the equation that links distance, force and work done. Give the unit for each quantity.

....

....

....

4 A force of 15 N moves a box a distance of 2 m.

Calculate the work done on the box.

....J

5 A wheelbarrow is moved 12 m. 240 J of energy is transferred.

Calculate the force on the wheelbarrow.

....N

6 A car is pushed with a force of 1 kN. 4.5 kJ of energy is transferred.

How far does the car move in metres?

....m

5 Forces and elasticity

Forces causing a change of shape

As well as causing changes in motion, **forces** can also cause a change of shape. Squashing, stretching or bending, or a combination of these, can cause an object to change shape.

When a force deforms an object, the change in shape may be permanent, as in the case of squashing a drinks can. However, the deformation of other objects may only be temporary (e.g. when stretching a band or bending a long bow). They return to their original shape when the force is removed.

Objects that return to their original shape after being deformed are made of elastic material.

Rubber is an elastic material so it can be used to make a catapult:
- The original length of the rubber band on the catapult is 18 cm.
- When stretched, the rubber band is 28 cm long.
- Band's increase in length = 28 − 18 = 10 cm.

This increase in length is also known as the **extension**.

extension = stretched length − original length

A neck pillow made of polyurethane foam can be used to provide comfort during a long journey:
- Polyurethane foam is an elastic material.
- Your head, resting on the pillow, may cause a compression of about 1 cm, but the pillow returns to its original shape after use.

compression = original thickness − compressed thickness

Hooke's law

The extension of some elastic materials doubles when the stretching force applied is doubled. These materials are said to obey Hooke's law.

The force and extension are linked by the equation below:

$$F = ke \quad \text{where}$$

F is the force, in newtons (N)

k is the spring constant, in newtons per metre (N/m)

e is the extension, in metres (m)

The spring constant tells you how much force is required to extend a material by 1 m.

Up to the elastic limit, some objects obey Hooke's law, $F = ke$. If the extension-against-force graph for a material is a straight line that passes through the origin (0, 0), the material obeys Hooke's law.

Calculating work done

A force that stretches (or compresses) an elastic object does work and elastic potential energy is stored in the object. Provided the object is not inelastically deformed, the work done is equal to the elastic potential energy stored in the object.

You can calculate the elastic potential energy stored in an object using the equation below:

$$E_e = \tfrac{1}{2}ke^2 \quad \text{where}$$

E_e is the elastic potential energy, in joules (J)

k is the spring constant, in newtons per metre (N/m)

e is the extension, in metres (m)

A spring with a spring constant of 2.5 N/m extends from 20 cm to 40 cm. Calculate the elastic potential energy stored in the spring when it extends.

List the information known about the spring.

Spring constant = 2.5 N/m

Extension = 40 − 20 = 20 cm

Extension = 0.2 m

Substitute these values into the equation for elastic potential energy.

$$E_e = \tfrac{1}{2}ke^2 = \tfrac{1}{2} \times 2.5 \times 0.2^2$$

$$E_e = 0.05 \, \text{J}$$

Forces and elasticity

Forces causing a change of shape

1 The original length of a spring is 20 cm. When a force is applied to the spring, its length changes to 60 cm.

Calculate the extension of the spring in metres.

.... m

2 A sponge is 5 cm thick. When it is squeezed, it becomes 1 cm thick.

Calculate the compression of the sponge.

.... cm

Hooke's law

3 In words, write the equation that links extension, force and spring constant. Give the unit for each quantity.

....

....

4 The graph shows the force and extension for an elastic object.

How does the graph show that the material obeys Hooke's law?

....

Calculating work done

5 An elastic band 10 cm in length is stretched. Its final length is 40 cm. The spring constant of the elastic band is 32 N/m.

Calculate the elastic potential energy stored in the stretched band.

.... J

6 20 J of elastic potential energy are stored in a spring, which has a spring constant of 2.5 N/m.

Calculate the extension of the spring in metres.

.... m

7 A spring has an initial length of 5 cm. 15 J of elastic potential energy are stored in the spring when it is stretched. The spring constant of the spring is 50 N/m.

Calculate the final length of the spring in centimetres. Give your answer to 2 significant figures.

.... cm

5 Levers, moments and gears

Levers

A **lever** enables a much greater turning force to be applied to a load than a person could exert with their bare hands.

The turning force generated by a lever is much larger than the effort if the load is much closer to the fulcrum than the effort.

An effort force turns a lever clockwise or anticlockwise. The effort force has to be moved through a much greater distance than the load moves.

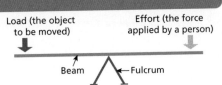

Load (the object to be moved)   Effort (the force applied by a person)

Beam   Fulcrum

The turning force exerted on a load can be increased if:
- the distance from the effort force to the fulcrum is increased
- the distance from the load to the fulcrum is reduced
- the size of the effort force is increased.

Moments

The turning effect of a force is called the **moment** and is calculated using the following equation:

$M = Fd$ where

M is the moment, in newton metres (Nm)

F is the size of the force, in newtons (N)

d is the distance from the force to the fulcrum, in metres (m)

In this diagram, the effort force applied to the screwdriver creates a clockwise turning effect, which causes the lid of the paint tin to be levered off. This turning effect can be increased if a larger force is exerted or a longer screwdriver is used.

Effort force applied to the screwdriver is 10 N

Rim of the tin acts as the fulcrum

Distance from the rim of the tin to where the effort force is applied to the screwdriver is 0.16 m

PAINT

So, moment = 10 × 0.16 = 1.6 Nm

Moments can be demonstrated with a model see-saw by balancing a metre rule on a triangular wooden block placed on a table. The wooden block acts as the fulcrum.

1 N weight

A 1 N weight is placed on the metre rule, 0.4 m from the fulcrum. The weight pushes down on the metre rule causing it to rotate clockwise.

clockwise moment = 1 × 0.4 = 0.4 Nm

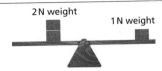

2 N weight

1 N weight

A 2 N weight is moved along the rule until it balances. The distance from the 2 N weight to the fulcrum is 0.2 m. The 2 N weight made the metre rule rotate in an anticlockwise direction until it was balanced. The rule is balanced as the two moments acting are equal in size and opposite in direction.

anticlockwise moment = 2 × 0.2 = 0.4 Nm

Gears

Machines can use **gears** to increase or decrease the rotational effects of a force.

If the larger wheel has twice the radius of the smaller wheel, the turning effect from the larger wheel will be twice that of the smaller wheel. The larger wheel can be called a **force multiplier**.

A gear with a radius of 0.2 m is turned by a smaller gear with a radius of 0.01 m. The moment of the smaller gear is 15 Nm. Calculate the moment of the larger gear.

$F = \dfrac{M}{d} = \dfrac{15}{0.01} = 1500\,N$ Begin by calculating the force of the smaller gear.

Use this force to calculate the moment of the larger gear.

$M = Fd = 1500 \times 0.2$ The moment of the larger gear is 20 times that of the smaller gear.
$M = 300\,Nm$

Levers, moments and gears

Levers

1 Label the diagram using these words:

| Load | Effort | Fulcrum |

2 State **three** ways in which the turning force on a load can be increased.

....

....

....

Moments

3 In words, write the equation that links distance, force and moment. Give the unit for each quantity.

....

....

4 An effort force of 7.5 N is applied to the end of the screwdriver to open the tin. The distance from the rim of the tin to the effort force is 0.3 m.

Calculate the moment of the force.

.... Nm

5 In the diagram, the distance from the handle to the hinge on the door is 0.75 m.

The turning effect is 11.25 Nm.

Calculate the force taken to open the door.

.... N

Gears

6 A gear with a radius of 0.4 m is turned by a smaller gear with a radius of 0.1 m. The moment of the larger gear is 150 Nm.

Calculate the moment of the smaller gear.

.... Nm

Pressure in a fluid and atmospheric pressure

Pressure in fluids

Fluids can be either liquids or gases. The pressure at the surface of a fluid can be calculated using the following equation:

$$P = \frac{F}{A}$$

where

P is the pressure, in pascals (Pa)

F is the force normal to a surface, in newtons (N)

A is the area, in metres squared (m²)

A fluid is a liquid or a gas.

HT Pressure in a liquid is caused by the liquid particles exerting forces on the container walls. Liquid pressure increases as depth increases (owing to more liquid pushing down from above).

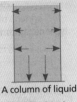

A column of liquid

Liquids cannot be compressed so at deep levels the liquid pushes harder on the container walls.

If you put holes in a container and keep topping up the water, the liquid pressure creates water jets. The bottom jet comes out with the most force.

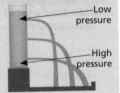

Low pressure

High pressure

HT Calculating pressure in fluids

The pressure due to a column of liquid can be calculated using the following equation:

$$P = h\rho g$$

where

P is the pressure, in pascals (Pa)

h is the height of the column, in metres (m)

ρ is the density of the liquid, in kilograms per cubic metre (kg/m³)

g is the gravitational field strength, in newtons per kilogram (N/kg)

The depth of water in a swimming pool is 2.5 m. The density of water is 1000 kg/m³. The gravitational field strength on Earth is 9.8 N/kg. Calculate the pressure exerted by the water on the bottom of the pool.

List the information given in the question.

Height = 2.5 m
Density = 1000 kg/m³
Gravitational field strength = 9.8 N/kg

Substitute these values into the equation for pressure.

$P = h\rho g = 2.5 \times 1000 \times 9.8$
$P = 24\,500\,Pa$

Atmospheric pressure

The atmosphere is a band of gas surrounding the Earth. The gas, usually called 'air', is mostly made up of nitrogen and oxygen molecules. Air molecules move very fast but cannot escape the Earth's gravity.

The gas pressure exerted by air molecules is called **atmospheric pressure**, which is measured with a barometer.

Atmospheric pressure decreases at higher altitudes. Air closer to the Earth's surface is squashed by the weight of the atmosphere above. Every breath taken at the top of Mount Everest contains less than a third of the oxygen molecules that the human body needs to function normally. This can cause altitude sickness so mountaineers take oxygen cylinders.

Atmospheric pressure at a specific location varies depending on the weather. In London, it typically ranges from 97 000 N/m² to 104 000 N/m².

Air molecules pushed closer together at sea level (where atmospheric pressure is about 100 000 N/m²)

Air molecules more spread apart at high altitude (on a high mountain atmospheric pressure may be just 30 000 N/m²)

RETRIEVE 5 Pressure in a fluid and atmospheric pressure

Pressure in fluids

1 In words, write the equation that links area, force and pressure. Give the unit for each variable in the equation.

_____

_____

_____

2 The air in a balloon exerts a force of 1.5 N. The area of the walls of the balloon is 0.8 m².

Calculate the pressure exerted by the air in the balloon.

_____ Pa

3 **HT** Explain why the pressure in a column of liquid increases with depth.

_____

_____

_____

_____

HT Calculating pressure in fluids

4 The density of water is 1000 kg/m³. A bath tub with a depth of 0.7 m is filled with water.

Calculate the pressure exerted by the water on the bottom of the bath tub. Take the gravitational field strength to be 9.8 N/kg.

_____ Pa

Atmospheric pressure

5 Explain why atmospheric pressure is greater at sea level than at the top of a mountain.

_____

_____

_____

_____

5 Distance, speed and velocity

Distance and displacement

The **distance** an object travels is the total number of metres (or kilometres or miles) travelled. Distance is a **scalar** quantity as it only has magnitude. In this image, this is shown by the red dotted line.

The **displacement** of an object is the distance moved in a straight line from the start to the end of the journey. Displacement is a **vector** quantity as it has both magnitude and direction. In this image, this is shown by the solid green line.

The difference between distance and displacement

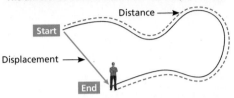

Speed

The **speed** of an object is a measure of how fast it is moving.

To work out the speed of any moving object, you need to know:
- the **distance** it travels
- the **time** it takes to travel that distance.

Typical values of speed

Walking	1.5 m/s
Running	3 m/s
Cycling	6 m/s

Calculating distance

Distance can be calculated using the following equation:

$$s = vt \quad \text{where}$$

s is the distance, in metres (m)

v is the speed, in metres per second (m/s)

t is the time, in seconds (s)

The slope of a **distance–time graph** represents the speed of an object. The steeper the slope, the greater the speed.

The graph below shows:
1 a stationary person
2 a person moving at a constant speed of 2 m/s
3 a person moving at a constant speed of 3 m/s.

A person walks at a speed of 1.5 m/s for 2 hours. Calculate the distance travelled in kilometres.

Begin by listing the information given in the question.

Speed = 1.5 m/s
Time = 2 × 60 × 60 = 7200 s

Substitute these values into the equation for distance.

$s = vt = 1.5 \times 7200$
$s = 10800 \, \text{m} = 10.8 \, \text{km}$

N.B. The vertical axis shows distance from a fixed point (0), not total distance travelled.

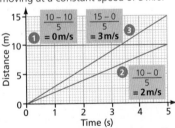

Velocity

Velocity and speed aren't the same thing. The velocity of a moving object describes its speed in a given direction.

Velocity is a vector quantity as it has both magnitude and direction.

Velocity of the car is 40 km/h East

Velocity of the car is 40 km/h South

HT If an object is travelling at a constant speed in a circle, its direction is constantly changing. This means that the object's velocity is also constantly changing.

If the vehicles on a roundabout travel at a constant speed, the velocity is **not** constant because the direction of the vehicles is constantly changing.

⑤ Distance, speed and velocity

Distance and displacement

1 What is the difference between distance and displacement?

Speed

2 State the **two** quantities that are needed in order to determine the speed of an object.

3 Complete the table to show typical values of speed for the activities.

Walking	.... m/s
Running	.... m/s
Cycling	.... m/s

Calculating distance

4 In words, write the equation which links distance, speed and time. Give the unit for each quantity in the equation.

5 An athlete runs at a speed of 3.5 m/s for 30 minutes.

How far does the athlete travel in this time?
Give your answer in kilometres.

.... km

6 A cyclist travels 21.6 kilometres in one hour.

Calculate the speed of the cyclist in metres per second.

.... m/s

Velocity

7 Explain why the velocity of an object travelling in a circle is changing, even if the object is travelling at a constant speed.

5 Acceleration

Calculating acceleration

The **acceleration** of an object is the rate at which its velocity changes. It is a measure of how quickly an object speeds up or slows down.

To work out the acceleration of any moving object, you need to know:
- the change in velocity
- the time taken for this change in velocity.

Acceleration can be calculated using the following equation:

$$a = \frac{\Delta v}{t} \quad \text{where}$$

a is the acceleration, in metres per second squared (m/s²)
Δv is the change in velocity, in metres per second (m/s)
t is the time, in seconds (s)

Deceleration is a negative acceleration. It describes an object that is slowing down. It is calculated using the same formula as above.

If the **acceleration is uniform**, the following equation can also be used to calculate acceleration:

$$v^2 - u^2 = 2as$$
$$\text{Rearranging gives: } a = \frac{(v^2 - u^2)}{2s}$$
where

v is the final velocity, in metres per second (m/s)
u is the initial velocity, in metres per second (m/s)
a is the acceleration, in metres per second squared (m/s²)
s is the distance, in metres (m)

a) A car starts from rest and accelerates to a velocity of 10 m/s. This takes 5 seconds. Calculate the acceleration of the car.

List the information known about the car.

Initial velocity = 0 m/s
Final velocity = 10 m/s
Velocity change = final velocity – initial velocity = 10 m/s
Time = 5 seconds

Substitute the values into the equation to calculate acceleration.

$$a = \frac{\Delta v}{t} = \frac{10}{5}$$
$$a = 2 \text{ m/s}^2$$

b) A car starts from rest and accelerates to a velocity of 8 m/s. In this time, the car travels a distance of 15 m. Calculate its acceleration.

List the information known about the car.

Initial velocity = 0 m/s
Final velocity = 8 m/s
Distance travelled = 15 m

Substitute these values into the equation for acceleration.

$$a = \frac{(v^2 - u^2)}{2s} = \frac{(8^2 - 0^2)}{2 \times 15}$$
$$a = 2.13 \text{ m/s}^2$$

Velocity–time graphs

The slope of a **velocity–time graph** represents the acceleration of the object. The steeper the slope, the greater the acceleration.

HT The area underneath the line in a velocity–time graph represents the total distance travelled.

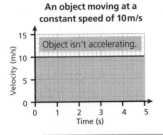

An object moving at a constant speed of 10 m/s

Object isn't accelerating.

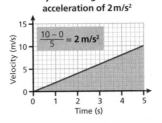

An object moving at a constant acceleration of 2 m/s²

$\frac{10 - 0}{5} = 2 \text{ m/s}^2$

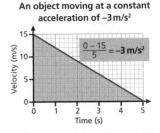

An object moving at a constant acceleration of –3 m/s²

$\frac{0 - 15}{5} = -3 \text{ m/s}^2$

The gradient of a velocity-time graph is equal to the acceleration of the object.

Acceleration

Calculating acceleration

1 Define the term 'acceleration' and give the units that it is measured in.

....

....

2 In words, write the equation that links acceleration, change in velocity and time.

....

3 A sprinter increases their velocity from 2 m/s to 8 m/s in a time of 6 seconds.

Calculate the acceleration of the sprinter.

.... m/s²

4 A car accelerates at a rate of 2 m/s² for 15 seconds.

If the car starts from rest, what is its final velocity?

.... m/s

Velocity–time graphs

5 State the quantity represented by:

a) the gradient ....

HT **b)** the area under a velocity–time graph ....

6 **a)** Plot a velocity–time graph of the data below.

Time (s)	Velocity (m/s)
0	0
5	2
10	4
15	6
20	6

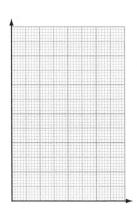

b) Use your graph to determine the acceleration of the object over the first 15 seconds.

.... m/s²

HT **c)** Use your graph to determine the total distance travelled by the object.

.... m

⑤ Newton's laws of motion

Newton's first law

Newton's first law of motion states that an object will remain stationary or remain travelling at the same speed, in the same direction, unless acted upon by an unbalanced force.

The forces acting on a stationary car are balanced.	If the forces acting on a moving car are equal, the car will remain travelling at the same speed in the same direction.
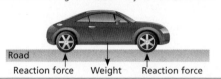 Road — Reaction force Weight Reaction force	 5000 N ← → 5000 N

Newton's second law

Newton's second law states that an object will accelerate when acted on by an **unbalanced** force.

The magnitude of the acceleration is directly proportional to the resultant force acting on the object: $a \propto F$

In other words, if the resultant force doubles, the acceleration will also double.

We can also say that acceleration is inversely proportional to the mass of the object: $a \propto \dfrac{1}{m}$

In other words, if the mass of the object doubles, the acceleration halves.

Putting these two relationships together gives the equation for Newton's second law:

$F = ma$ where
F is the force, in newtons (N)
m is the mass, in kilograms (kg)
a is the acceleration, in metres per second squared (m/s²)

Resultant force
→
40 N

Thrust force
100 N

Friction
60 N

The forces on the truck are unbalanced, so it will accelerate in the direction of the resultant force.

A car of mass 1200 kg accelerates at 3 m/s². Calculate the resultant force acting on the car.

List the information known about the car.

Mass = 1200 kg   Acceleration = 3 m/s²

Substitute the values into the equation for force.

$F = ma = 1200 \times 3$

$F = 3600$ N

Newton's third law

Newton's third law states that for every action force, there is an equal and opposite reaction force.

These pairs of forces must:
- act on different bodies
- act in opposite directions
- act along the same line
- be of the same type (e.g. both gravitational forces)
- be of the same magnitude.

The Earth pulls the Moon towards it with a gravitational force. The Moon also pulls the Earth towards it, also with a gravitational force. Notice that the arrows are drawn along the same line and are of equal length. They are drawn pointing in opposite directions.

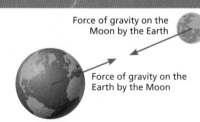

Force of gravity on the Moon by the Earth

Force of gravity on the Earth by the Moon

This shows that the forces act along the same line, are equal in magnitude and that the gravitational forces of the Earth and Moon are acting in opposite directions.

⑤ Newton's laws of motion

Newton's first law

1 State Newton's first law of motion.

2 Use Newton's first law to explain why a book resting on a table is stationary.

Newton's second law

3 State Newton's second law.

4 A lorry with a mass of 20 tonnes accelerates at a rate of $2\,m/s^2$.

Calculate the force required for this acceleration. 1 tonne = 1000 kg.

.... N

5 A cyclist and a bike have a combined mass of 100 kg.

If a force of 500 N is applied, calculate the acceleration of the cyclist and bike.

.... m/s^2

Newton's third law

6 State Newton's third law.

7 List the **five** features of the pairs of forces in Newton's third law.

5 Stopping distance and reaction time

Stopping distance

In order to bring a moving car to stop, the driver must apply the brakes. Along with frictional forces, this causes the car to decelerate.

To apply the brakes, the driver must first **react** to a stimulus, such as a traffic light turning red. The average person has a reaction time of 0.2–0.9 seconds. In this time, the car is still travelling. The distance that the car moves during this time is called the **thinking distance**.

As soon as the driver applies the brakes, the car will begin to decelerate and come to a stop. The distance travelled in the time this takes is called the **braking distance**.

The faster the vehicle is moving, for a given braking force, the longer the braking distance. Learner drivers are required to know the stopping distances of a vehicle at different speeds as given in the Highway Code.

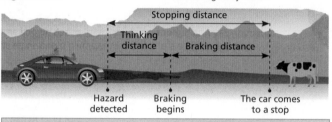

Stopping distance = thinking distance + braking distance

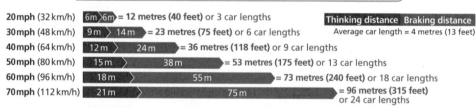

	Thinking distance	Braking distance
	Average car length = 4 metres (13 feet)	

20mph (32 km/h) 6m 6m = **12 metres (40 feet)** or 3 car lengths
30mph (48 km/h) 9m 14m = **23 metres (75 feet)** or 6 car lengths
40mph (64 km/h) 12m 24m = **36 metres (118 feet)** or 9 car lengths
50mph (80 km/h) 15m 38m = **53 metres (175 feet)** or 13 car lengths
60mph (96 km/h) 18m 55m = **73 metres (240 feet)** or 18 car lengths
70mph (112 km/h) 21m 75m = **96 metres (315 feet)** or 24 car lengths

Reaction time and thinking distance

The longer the reaction time, the longer the thinking distance.

The reaction time for a driver can be affected by:
- tiredness – if the driver is tired, their reaction time will increase
- taking drugs – if a driver is taking medication or illegal substances, it may increase reaction time

- drinking alcohol – this also increases reaction time
- distractions, such as the driver using a handheld mobile phone (which is now illegal in the UK) or children playing in the back of a car, can increase reaction time.

Factors affecting braking distance

The faster the speed of the vehicle, the greater the braking distance.

Other factors affecting the braking distance include:
- the condition of the road – wet or icy roads can reduce the friction between the tyres and the road surface, increasing the braking distance
- the condition of the vehicle – worn brakes or worn tyres increase the braking distance.

A vehicle travelling at a greater speed requires a greater braking force to bring it to a stop. This means a greater deceleration, which increases the temperature of the brakes owing to increased frictional forces. This can cause the brakes to overheat.

Factors affecting the thinking distance relate to the driver. Factors affecting the braking distance relate to the weather, the vehicle or the road conditions.

5 Stopping distance and reaction time

Stopping distance

1 State the average human reaction time. .... s

2 **a)** What is meant by the term 'thinking distance'?

....

....

b) What is meant by the term 'braking distance'?

....

....

3 The thinking distance for a vehicle travelling at 30 mph is 9 m. The braking distance is 14 m. Calculate the stopping distance for the vehicle.

.... m

Reaction time and thinking distance

4 Give **three** factors that increase a driver's reaction time.

....

....

....

Factors affecting braking distance

5 Give **three** factors that increase the braking distance of a vehicle.

....

....

....

6 Explain why a large deceleration can cause the brakes of a vehicle to overheat.

....

....

....

5 Momentum

HT Momentum

Momentum is a measure of the state of motion of an object. It depends on the **mass** of the object (in kg) and the **velocity** of the object (in m/s).

If a car moves with a greater velocity, it will have more momentum provided its mass hasn't changed. However, a moving truck with a greater mass may have more momentum than the car even if its velocity is less.

Momentum is calculated using the equation below:

$$p = mv \quad \text{where}$$

p is the momentum, in kilogram metres per second (kg m/s)

m is the mass, in kilograms (kg)

v is the velocity, in metres per second (m/s)

a) Calculate the momentum of a car of mass 1200 kg that is moving at a velocity of 30 m/s.

List the information known about the car.

Mass = 1200 kg   Velocity = 30 m/s

Substitute these values into the equation for momentum.

$p = mv = 1200 \times 30 = 36\,000$ kg m/s

b) A truck has a mass of 4000 kg. Calculate the truck's velocity if it has a momentum of 36 000 kg m/s.

Rearrange the equation to make velocity the subject and substitute the values into it.

$v = \dfrac{p}{m} = \dfrac{36\,000}{4000}$ Notice that since the truck has a greater mass than the car in part a),

$v = 9$ m/s   it can move at a slower speed and still have the same momentum.

HT Conservation of momentum

Provided that two objects are in a **closed system** when they collide, the momentum before the collision will be equal to the momentum after the collision. This is called the law of **conservation of momentum**.

Toy car A has a mass of 3 kg and is moving at a velocity of 2 m/s. It collides with toy car B, which has a mass of 3 kg and is stationary. Upon colliding, the toy cars stick together and move off. Calculate the velocity of the toy cars after the collision.

Work out the total momentum before the collision.

Toy car A = 3 × 2 = 6 kg m/s
Toy car B = 3 × 0 = 0 kg m/s } 6 + 0 = 6 kg m/s

As momentum is conserved, the momentum of the toy cars after the collision must also be 6 kg m/s. The total mass is 6 kg. Put the values into the equation for velocity.

$v = \dfrac{p}{m} = \dfrac{6}{6} = 1$ m/s

So, the toy cars move off with a velocity of 1 m/s.

Sketching diagrams of the situation before and after the collision can help.

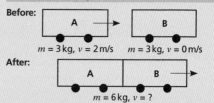

Before:
A → B
$m = 3$ kg, $v = 2$ m/s $m = 3$ kg, $v = 0$ m/s

After:
A B →
$m = 6$ kg, $v = ?$

HT Force and change of momentum

Acceleration = $\dfrac{\text{change in velocity}}{\text{time}}$

Force = mass × acceleration

Therefore: Force = $\dfrac{\text{mass} \times \text{change in velocity}}{\text{time}}$

And since mass × change in velocity is equal to momentum:

Force = $\dfrac{\text{change in momentum}}{\text{time}}$

Crumple zone   Air bag   Seat belts

The final equation above explains why modern vehicles have safety features, such as seat belts, crumple zones and air bags. In a collision, the momentum of a moving object will be reduced to zero. If the time for this change in momentum to occur is short, there will be a large force felt on the body. However, if the time for the change in momentum can be increased, the force on the body will be significantly reduced.

HT Momentum

1 In words, write the equation that links mass, momentum and velocity.

_____

2 A rugby player has a mass of 80 kg and is running at a velocity of 3 m/s.

Calculate the momentum of the rugby player.

_____ kg m/s

3 A car has a mass of 1500 kg and is moving with a momentum of 15 000 kg m/s.

Calculate the velocity of the car.

_____ m/s

HT Conservation of momentum

4 State the law of conservation of momentum.

_____

_____

_____

HT Force and change of momentum

5 Why do modern cars have crumple zones as part of their design? Use ideas about forces and changes of momentum in your answer.

_____

_____

_____

_____

6 A car passenger has a mass of 60 kg. The car is travelling at a velocity of 10 m/s. The time taken for the passenger to come to a stop in a collision is 0.2 seconds without a seat belt and 2 seconds when wearing a seat belt.

Calculate the force experienced by the passenger when the car comes to a stop:

a) if they are **not** wearing a seat belt

_____ N

b) if they are wearing a seat belt.

_____ N

Transverse waves, longitudinal waves and reflection

A wave is a disturbance that travels from one point to another, transferring energy.

Transverse waves (e.g. ripples on a water surface) transfer energy in a direction that is perpendicular (at right angles) to the oscillations (vibrations).

Longitudinal waves (e.g. sound waves) also transfer energy, but the direction of oscillation is parallel to the direction of energy transfer.

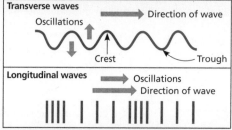

Wave	Transverse	Longitudinal	Carries energy	Can travel through a vacuum	Can be reflected
Light	✓	✗	✓	✓	✓
Sound	✗	✓	✓	✗	✓
Water surface	✓	✗	✓	✗	✓

When light strikes a surface, it changes direction. This is called **reflection**.

The **normal** is a line that is perpendicular to the reflecting surface at the point of incidence. The normal is used to calculate the angles of incidence and reflection.

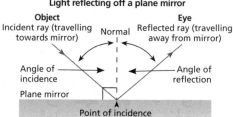

Angle of incidence = Angle of reflection

Wave terms and calculations

Amplitude: the maximum displacement of a point on a wave away from its undisturbed position (i.e. the distance in metres from the undisturbed position to the crest, or from the undisturbed position to the trough)

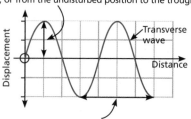

Wavelength: the distance in metres from a point on one wave to the equivalent point on the next wave

The **frequency** is measured in hertz, where 1 hertz means one complete wave passes a given point every second. The **time period** is the time taken for one wave to pass a given point.

$$T = \frac{1}{f} \quad \text{which can be rearranged to} \quad f = \frac{1}{T}$$

where

T is the time period, in seconds (s)

f is the frequency, in hertz (Hz)

The equation below calculates the speed of a wave.

$$v = f\lambda \quad \text{where}$$

v is the wave speed, in metres per second (m/s)

f is the frequency, in hertz (Hz)

λ is the wavelength, in metres (m)

a) Calculate the frequency of a wave with a time period of 5 seconds.

$f = \frac{1}{T} = \frac{1}{5}$

$= 0.2\,Hz$

b) Calculate the speed of a wave with a wavelength of 50cm and a frequency of 10Hz.

$v = f\lambda = 10 \times 0.5$ Convert the wavelength to metres.

$v = 5\,m/s$

Types and properties of waves

Transverse waves, longitudinal waves and reflection

1 Give an example of:

a) a transverse wave ....

b) a longitudinal wave ....

2 Label the diagram with the words 'trough' and 'crest'.

Direction of
travel of the wave

3 A ray of light is incident on a plane mirror. The angle of incidence is 35°.

What is the angle of reflection of the light ray? .... °

Wave terms and calculations

4 What is meant by the 'amplitude' of a wave?

....

....

5 Define the 'frequency' of a wave and state the unit in which it is measured.

....

....

6 A wave has a time period of 10 seconds.

Calculate the frequency of the wave.

.... Hz

7 In words, write the equation that links frequency, wavelength and wave speed.

....

8 A wave with a frequency of 500 Hz has a wavelength of 0.1 cm.

Calculate the speed of the wave in metres per second.

.... m/s

9 A wave is travelling at 3×10^6 m/s with a frequency of 3000 Hz.

Calculate the wavelength of the wave. Give your answer in standard form.

.... m

Sound waves and waves for detection and exploration

ⓗ Sound waves

Sound travels as waves. The waves are produced when something mechanical vibrates backwards and forwards. The quality of a note depends on the waveform.

Remember, if a wave is refracted, it changes direction when it passes through one substance into another.

Sound can't travel through a vacuum. It can be:
- **reflected** off hard surfaces to produce echoes
- **refracted** when it passes into a different medium or substance.

Outside the range of 20 Hz to 20 000 Hz, the human ear cannot detect the sound waves.

ⓗ Ultrasound waves

Ultrasound is sound waves of frequencies greater than 20 000 Hz, i.e. above the upper limit of the hearing range for humans. Electronic systems produce electrical oscillations, which are used to generate the ultrasonic waves.

As ultrasonic waves pass from one medium or substance into another, they are partially reflected at the boundary. The time taken for the reflections is a measure of how far away the boundary is. Some uses of ultrasound are shown below.

Detecting flaws and cracks	Pre-natal scanning	Cleaning delicate objects
Some of the ultrasound waves are reflected back by the flaw or crack within the structure.	This method is safe with little risk to the patient or baby.	The vibrations caused by the ultrasound waves can be used within a liquid to dislodge dirt particles from the surface of an object. There is no danger of breakage and no need to take the object apart.

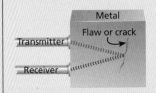

Metal
Flaw or crack
Transmitter
Receiver

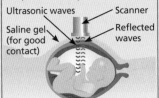

Ultrasonic waves — Scanner
Saline gel (for good contact)
Reflected waves

Ring
Transmitter
Cleaning liquid

ⓗ Seismic waves

Seismic waves are from earthquakes. There are two types of seismic wave: P-waves and S-waves.

The path of these waves provide evidence of the Earth's structure and the size of its core.

P-waves:
- are longitudinal
- can travel through solids and liquids.

Crust
Mantle
Solid inner core
Liquid outer core
P-waves can pass through Earth's core

S-waves:
- are transverse
- can only travel through solids.

S-waves cannot pass through Earth's liquid outer core

ⓗ Echo sounding

Sound waves with a high frequency can be used to locate objects in deep water and to measure the depth of water.

A transmitter sends out a sound wave. The time taken for the wave to reflect and reach a detector is measured. Since distance = speed × time, the depth of water can be determined.

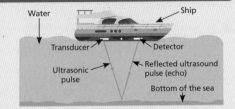

Water — Ship
Transducer — Detector
Ultrasonic pulse
Reflected ultrasound pulse (echo)
Bottom of the sea

Sound waves and waves for detection and exploration

HT Sound waves

1 State the range of human hearing in hertz.

HT Ultrasound waves

2 List **three** uses of ultrasound waves.

3 Explain how ultrasound waves can be used in medical imaging.

HT Seismic waves

4 How do P-waves and S-waves differ? Refer to their wave type and the substances they can travel through.

5 Explain how seismic waves can be used to provide evidence for the structure of the Earth and for the size of its core.

HT Echo sounding

6 A sonar transmitter on a boat sends an ultrasound signal towards the sea bed. 0.2 seconds later, the pulse is detected by a detector on the boat. The speed of a sound wave in water is 1500 m/s.

Calculate the depth of the sea.

_____ m

Types and properties of electromagnetic waves

Electromagnetic waves

Electromagnetic radiations are disturbances in an electric field. They travel as waves and transfer energy from one place to another.

All types of electromagnetic radiation travel at the same speed through a vacuum.

Each type of electromagnetic radiation has a **different wavelength** and a **different frequency**. Together, they form the **electromagnetic spectrum**, shown below.

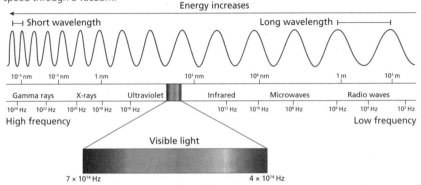

When radiation is absorbed by a substance:
- the energy is absorbed and makes the substance heat up
- it may create an alternating current of the same frequency as the radiation.

Different wavelengths of electromagnetic radiation are **reflected, absorbed** or **transmitted** in different ways by different substances and surfaces.

Visible light is the only part of the electromagnetic spectrum that can be seen by the human eye.

White light is made up of different colours. The colours are **refracted** by different amounts as they pass through a prism:
- Red light is refracted the least.
- Violet light is refracted the most.

🔴 Properties of electromagnetic waves

Electromagnetic waves refract when they cross the boundary between two transparent materials. They change direction owing to a change in speed.

The diagrams show an experiment in which a red laser beam is directed at a glass block. Light is a transverse wave, so the laser beam can be represented by rows of crests.

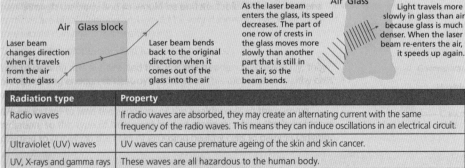

Radiation type	Property
Radio waves	If radio waves are absorbed, they may create an alternating current with the same frequency of the radio waves. This means they can induce oscillations in an electrical circuit.
Ultraviolet (UV) waves	UV waves can cause premature ageing of the skin and skin cancer.
UV, X-rays and gamma rays	These waves are all hazardous to the human body.
X-rays and gamma rays	These waves are ionising, which means they can cause mutations in body cells.

Types and properties of electromagnetic waves

Electromagnetic waves

1 List the types of electromagnetic wave from longest wavelength to shortest wavelength.

....

....

2 Calculate the speed of blue light, given the following information.

Frequency = 7.0×10^{14} Hz

Wavelength = 4.3×10^{-7} m

Speed = frequency × wavelength

.... m/s

HT Properties of electromagnetic waves

3 Define the term 'refraction'.

....

4 List **three** parts of the electromagnetic spectrum that are hazardous to the human body.

....

5 Use the diagram to explain how radio waves can be used to induce electrical oscillations in an electrical circuit.

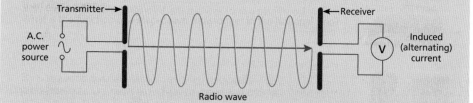

....

....

....

6 X-rays and gamma rays can both cause cancer in the human body. Explain how.

....

....

....

....

Uses and applications of electromagnetic waves

Uses and applications of electromagnetic waves

Electromagnetic waves	Uses	Effects
Radio waves	• Transmitting radio and TV signals between places across the Earth.	• High levels of exposure for short periods can increase body temperature, leading to tissue damage.
Microwaves	• Satellite communication networks and mobile phone networks (they can pass through the Earth's atmosphere). • Cooking – water molecules absorb microwaves, and heat up.	• May damage or kill cells because microwaves are absorbed by water in the cells, which heat up.
Infrared rays	• Grills, toasters and radiant heaters (e.g. electric fires). • Remote controls for televisions, etc. • Optical fibre communication.	• Absorbed by skin and felt as heat. • An excessive amount can cause burns.
Ultraviolet rays	• Security coding – special paint absorbs UV and emits visible light. • Sun tanning and sunbeds.	• Passes through skin to the tissues below. • High doses can kill cells. • A low dose can cause cancer.
X-rays	• Producing shadow pictures of bones and metals. • Treating certain cancers.	• Passes through soft tissues (some is absorbed). • High doses can kill cells. • A low dose can cause cancer.
Gamma rays	• Killing cancerous cells. • Killing bacteria on food and surgical instruments.	• Passes through soft tissues (some is absorbed). • High doses can kill cells. • A low dose can cause cancer.

Different parts of the electromagnetic spectrum have different uses. Radio waves and microwaves can be used for communication. X-rays and gamma rays can be used for medical imaging and treatment.

Uses and applications of electromagnetic waves

Uses and applications of electromagnetic waves

1 Draw lines to match the type of electromagnetic wave to its use.

Type of electromagnetic wave	Use
Radio waves	Remote controls for televisions
Microwaves	Transmitting TV signals
Infrared radiation	Producing shadow pictures of bones
Ultraviolet radiation	Satellite communications
X-rays	Killing bacteria on food
Gamma rays	Security coding

2 Explain why exposure to microwaves can damage cells in the body.

....

....

3 How are X-rays and gamma rays hazardous to the human body?

....

....

....

....

4 Sunbeds in tanning studios use ultraviolet radiation.

Explain why care must be taken when using sunbeds.

....

....

....

....

Lenses and visible light

Diverging and converging lenses

A lens is a piece of transparent material that refracts light rays. There are two types of lens.

The different lenses have a different curvature, so parallel rays of light pass through them differently.

Diverging lens	Converging lens
A diverging lens is: • concave (thinnest at its centre) • represented in ray diagrams by this symbol:)(	A converging lens is: • convex (thickest at its centre) • represented in ray diagrams by this symbol: ↕
A concave lens refracts rays of light outwards at the two curved boundaries so they appear to come from one point, the focus (F). Only the ray which meets the lens at 90° will pass straight through the lens. The image produced by a diverging lens is **virtual** (it appears to come from behind the lens) and **upright**.	A double convex lens refracts rays of light inwards at the two curved boundaries so they meet at the focus. Only the ray which meets the lens at 90° will pass straight through the lens. The image produced by a converging lens depends on the distance of the object from the lens. If the distance from the object to the lens is less than the distance from the lens to the focus point (F), the image produced is **virtual**, **upright** and **enlarged**, e.g. in a magnifying glass. If the distance from the object and the lens is greater than the distance from the lens to the focus point, the image produced is **real**, **inverted** (upside down compared to the object) and **diminished**, e.g. in the human eye.

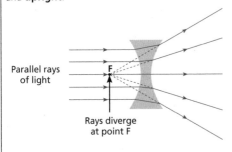

Parallel rays of light — F
Rays diverge at point F

Parallel rays of light — F
Rays diverge at point F

Magnification

Lenses can be used to produce a **magnification**. The magnification of a lens can be calculated using the equation:

$$\text{magnification} = \frac{\text{image size}}{\text{object size}}$$

An arrow with a height of 5cm is examined through a lens. The height of the image formed by the lens is 20cm. Calculate the magnification of the lens.

Magnification = $\frac{20}{5}$ = 4

There are no units for magnification as it is a ratio.

Visible light: reflection

The reflection of light by a mirror or another smooth surface (e.g. still water) is called **specular reflection**.

The reflection of light by an uneven surface (e.g. choppy water) is called **diffuse scattering**.

When you look in a mirror, your image is **virtual**.

Your image in a plane (flat) mirror is upright and the same height as you. But if you raise your right hand, the image's left hand is raised. The right side of an object appears on the left side of the image created by a plane mirror.

Specular reflection

Diffuse scattering

→ Incident ray
→ Reflected ray

(6) Lenses and visible light

Diverging and converging lenses

1 Draw symbols to show how each lens is shown in a ray diagram.

a) Diverging lens

b) Converging lens

2 Describe the image formed using a diverging lens.

....

....

3 Complete the diagram below to show how a converging lens focuses parallel rays of light.

Parallel rays
of light

Magnification

4 An object with a width of 2.5 cm is examined under a lens. The image produced by the lens has a width of 10 cm.

Calculate the magnification of the lens.

Magnification = ...

5 A lens has a magnification of ×10.

Calculate the height of a ladybird if the image is 5 cm tall.

.... cm

Visible light: reflection

6 Explain the difference between specular reflection and diffuse scattering.

....

....

....

....

6 Black body radiation

Emission and absorption of infrared radiation

All objects absorb and emit infrared radiation. The hotter the object, the more infrared radiation it emits in a given time.

A hot cup of coffee will emit more infrared radiation in a given time than a glass of water

Perfect black bodies and radiation

A **perfect black body** is an object that absorbs all of the incident radiation. It does **not** transmit or reflect any of the radiation it absorbs.

Good absorbers are also good emitters. A perfect black body will also be the best possible emitter. There are no objects that act as perfect black bodies; black holes and planets are assumed to be almost perfect black bodies.

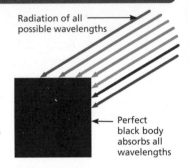

Radiation of all possible wavelengths

No wavelengths are reflected or transmitted

Perfect black body absorbs all wavelengths

HT An object that is at a constant temperature is absorbing and emitting infrared radiation at the same rate. If the temperature of an object increases, it is absorbing radiation at a faster rate than it is emitting it.

For example, as bread bakes, its temperature increases. This means that it is absorbing radiation at a faster rate than it is emitting it.

The temperature of the Earth depends on many factors including:
- the rates of absorption and emission of radiation
- reflection of radiation into space.

If it is a cloudy night, the temperature of the Earth remains higher than if it was a clear night. This is because the clouds reflect some of the infrared radiation lost by the Earth back to the surface and the Earth absorbs this radiation, increasing the temperature.

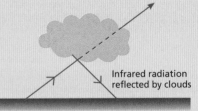

Infrared radiation reflected by clouds

Black body radiation

Emission and absorption of infrared radiation

1 What is the relationship between the temperature of an object and the amount of infrared radiation emitted in a given time?

Perfect black bodies and radiation

2 What is the meaning of the term 'perfect black body'?

3 Using ideas about infrared radiation, explain why a hot cup of tea cools down.

4 **HT** Give **two** factors that affect the temperature of the Earth.

5 **HT** The temperature of the Earth decreases at night time as it is not absorbing infrared radiation from the Sun.

Explain why clear nights on the side of the Earth at night are much cooler than cloudy nights.

(7) Magnetism

Poles and magnetic fields

A **magnet** is something that creates an invisible **magnetic field** in the space that surrounds it. All magnets have a north pole and a south pole.

Opposite poles of two magnets attract	Like poles of two magnets repel
The attractive force of two opposite poles is caused by the interaction of their fields and is called a **magnetic force**. Since it exists without the magnets touching, it is a non-contact force. 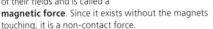	The magnetic force experienced between two north poles, or between two south poles, is a repulsive, non-contact force. 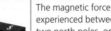

Iron filings can be used to show a magnetic field because iron is a magnetic material. They are pushed and pulled into the shape of the magnetic field. Other magnetic materials include nickel, steel, cobalt and neodymium.

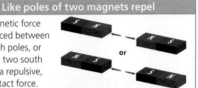

When a magnetised steel needle is placed on a piece of cork floating in a bowl of water, the needle's magnetic field interacts with the Earth's magnetic field. This makes the needle rotate so that one end points towards the Earth's North Pole. This end is called a north-seeking pole.

A suspended magnetised needle forms part of a compass. A navigation compass is used by sailors and hikers to find their way.

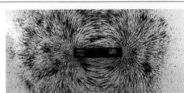

A smaller version of a compass, called a **plotting compass**, can be used to find out more about the shape of the magnetic field of a bar magnet. The red half of the needle gives the direction that the compass is pointing.

In a diagram, the magnetic field is represented by lines with arrows showing the direction a compass would point when placed at that position. Notice how the arrows on the magnetic field lines always point from north to south.

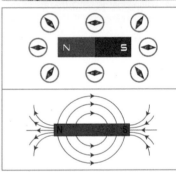

Types of magnetism

Permanent magnets keep their magnetic properties. Most contain the strongly magnetic materials of iron, nickel or cobalt.

Repeatedly stroking a steel nail with the north pole of a magnet in the direction shown by the arrows magnetises the nail. In this case, the point of the nail becomes a north pole, and the head becomes a south pole. A magnetised steel nail will retain its magnetism unless it is dropped or hit with a hammer.

Nail made of steel (iron mixed with carbon)

Inside the nail, each atom of iron acts like a tiny magnet. The atoms band together in a region within the nail, so their tiny magnets create magnetic fields with the same direction. These regions are called **domains**.

Stroking a steel nail with a magnet aligns its domains, giving it permanent magnetism.

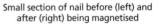
Small section of nail before (left) and after (right) being magnetised

Induced magnets are made from materials that become magnetic when placed in a magnetic field. There is always a force of attraction between a magnet and an induced magnet. Induced magnets lose their magnetism when removed from the magnetic field.

> Permanent magnets produce their own magnetic fields. Induced magnets only become magnetic when placed in a magnetic field.

⑦ Magnetism

Poles and magnetic fields

1 What are the **two** poles of a magnet called?

....

2 Magnetism is an example of a non-contact force.

Explain how this can be shown using two bar magnets.

....

....

....

....

3 What is meant by the term 'magnetic field'?

....

....

4 Iron is a magnetic material.

Name **two** other magnetic materials.

....

....

Types of magnetism

5 What is a permanent magnet? Give an example.

....

....

6 Explain how a steel nail can become magnetised.

....

....

....

7 What is an induced magnet?

....

....

....

7 Electromagnetism

Temporary magnets

A weak magnetic field can be created with a piece of wire and a battery. The wire is made of copper with a plastic coating.

When the switch in the circuit is open, no electric current flows and a magnetic field is not created so the plotting compass needles point north. 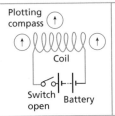	When the switch is closed, an electric current is flowing in the coil. The plotting compass needles have changed direction: the coil is now producing a magnetic field. It is an **electromagnet**. 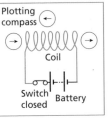

A very strong magnetic field, which can be switched on and off as desired, can be made with a long coil containing a core of soft iron. It is called a **solenoid**.

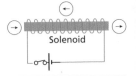

An iron-cored solenoid, carrying an electric current, creates a strong magnetic field.

Magnet	Type of magnet	Strength of field
Bar magnet	Permanent	Quite strong
Electromagnet with air core	Temporary	Weak
Solenoid with iron core	Temporary	Very strong

Advantages and applications of electromagnets

Most useful electromagnets consist of a coil, sometimes containing a soft iron core. When a battery is connected to the coil, it drives an electric current around it. This creates the magnetic field.

Three advantages of an electromagnet compared with a permanent magnet are:
- the magnetic field can be easily switched on or off by connecting or disconnecting the battery
- the electric current can be varied so the strength of the field can be controlled
- the direction of the field can be easily reversed by reversing the battery connections.

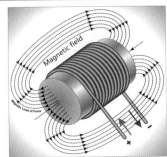

The magnetic field of an electromagnet can be switched on or off, can be made stronger or weaker, and made to change direction

Some of the uses of electromagnets include headphones, loudspeakers, electric bells, scrapyard cranes, data storage and magnetic locks.

Headphones Each earpiece in a set of headphones contains a permanent magnet and an electromagnet. The interaction between them causes the vibration that produces sound.	**Electric bells** The electric bell contains a coil wrapped around a U-shaped iron core. Pushing the switch connects the coil to a battery (not shown in the diagram). When the iron core becomes magnetised, it attracts the iron hammer, causing it to hit the gong. The process repeats itself, producing the ringing sound. 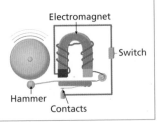

(7) Electromagnetism

Temporary magnetism

1 What is an electromagnet?

....

....

....

2 What is a solenoid?

....

3 Complete the table.

Magnet	Type of magnet	Strength of field
Bar magnet	....	Quite strong
Electromagnet with air core	Temporary	....
Solenoid with iron core	....	Very strong

Advantages and applications of electromagnets

4 List **three** advantages of electromagnets compared with a permanent magnet.

....

....

....

....

....

....

5 List **three** applications of electromagnets.

....

....

....

6 Explain how electromagnets are used in headphones.

....

....

....

....

7 Fleming's left-hand rule

The motor effect and factors affecting the force on a wire

The motor effect uses current to produce movement.

When a conductor (wire) carrying an electric current is placed in a magnetic field, the magnetic field formed around the wire interacts with the permanent magnetic field. This causes the wire to experience a force, which makes it move.

> The wire will **not** experience a force if it is parallel to the magnetic field.

How to increase the size of the force on the wire	How to reverse the direction of the force on the wire
• **Increase the size of the current** (e.g. have more cells) 	• **Reverse the direction of flow** of the current (e.g. turn the cell around) 
• **Increase the strength of the magnetic field** (e.g. have stronger magnets) 	• **Reverse the direction of the magnetic field** (e.g. swap the position of the north and south poles) 

HT Fleming's left-hand rule

Fleming's left-hand rule can be used to determine the relative orientation of the force, the magnetic field and the current on the wire in a magnetic field.

Hold your thumb, first finger and second finger at right angles to one another:
- Your thumb will point in the direction of the force (and so direction of movement) on the wire.
- Your first finger needs to be lined up with the magnetic field, from north to south.
- Your second finger needs to be lined up with the current, from positive to negative.

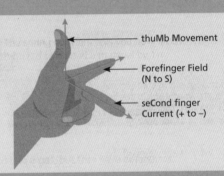

thuMb Movement

Forefinger Field (N to S)

seCond finger Current (+ to −)

HT Calculating the force on a current-carrying wire

For a current-carrying wire at right angles to a magnetic field:

$$F = BIL \text{ where}$$

F is the force, in newtons (N)
B is the magnetic flux density, in teslas (T)
I is the current, in amperes (A)
L is the length of the wire, in metres (m)

A current of 3A flows through a 1.5m long wire when it is placed in a magnetic field of flux density 0.5T. Calculate the force on the wire.

Substitute the given values into the formula for force.

$$F = BIL = 0.5 \times 3 \times 1.5$$
$$F = 2.25 \text{N}$$

You may need to rearrange the equation $F = BIL$ to make the unknown quantity the subject:

If the magnetic flux density is unknown		If the current is unknown		If the length of wire is unknown	
$F = BIL$		$F = BIL$		$F = BIL$	
$\dfrac{F}{IL} = B$	Divide both sides of the equation by IL.	$\dfrac{F}{BL} = I$	Divide both sides of the equation by BL.	$\dfrac{F}{BI} = L$	Divide both sides of the equation by BI.

⑦ Fleming's left-hand rule

The motor effect and factors affecting the force on a wire

1 What is meant by the 'motor effect'?

_____

_____

_____

_____

_____

2 State **two** ways in which the force on a wire in a magnetic field can be increased.

_____

_____

3 State **two** ways in which the direction of force on a wire on a magnetic field can be reversed.

_____

_____

HT Fleming's left-hand rule

4 The diagram shows a current-carrying wire placed in a magnetic field.

Use Fleming's left-hand rule to determine the direction that the wire will move.

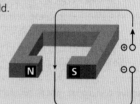

_____

_____

_____

_____

_____

HT Calculating the force on a current-carrying wire

5 In words, write the equation that links current, force, length and magnetic flux density.

_____

6 Calculate the force on a 2.5 m current-carrying wire that is placed in a magnetic field of flux density 1.5 T with a current of 10 A flowing through it.

_____ N

7 Electric motors and loudspeakers

Interacting magnetic fields

When two magnets are moved close enough for their magnetic fields to overlap, an interaction occurs. The interaction can result in either an attractive or a repulsive force.

A similar interaction occurs between a magnet and a magnetic field produced by a wire carrying an electric current.

> Motion caused by the interaction between a permanent magnet and an electromagnet is called the **motor effect**.

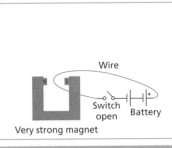

Wire

Switch open | Battery

Very strong magnet

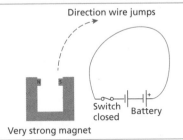

Direction wire jumps

Switch closed | Battery

Very strong magnet

When the switch is closed, electric current flows in the wire. The wire instantly jumps out of the magnet in the direction shown by the dashed red arrow.

HT The electric motor

The function of an electric motor is to create rotation. A battery (not shown) is connected to the coil, which becomes an electromagnet.

- The coil's magnetic field and the field produced by the magnets interact.
- The interaction creates an upward force on the left side of the coil. This is shown by the red arrow pointing upwards.
- The interaction also creates a downward force on the right side of the coil. This is shown by the red arrow pointing downwards.
- The upward and downward forces, shown by the red arrows, make the coil rotate clockwise.

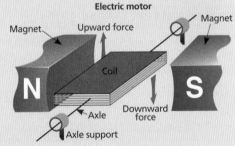

Electric motor

Magnet — Upward force — Magnet

Coil

Downward force

Axle

Axle support

Household appliances that are fitted with an electric motor include: washing machine; tumble dryer; microwave oven; electric tin opener; electric food mixer; electric fan.

HT Loudspeakers and headphones

Headphones contain small loudspeakers. Loudspeakers use the motor effect to create variations that result in the vibration of a cone, varying the air pressure inside the speakers and forming sound waves.

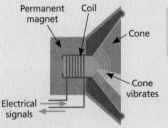

Permanent magnet | Coil

Cone

Cone vibrates

Electrical signals

The current in the coil of wire produces a magnetic field.

This magnetic field interacts with the permanent magnet, creating a force. This causes the cone to move outwards.

The direction of the current is reversed. This reverses the direction of the electromagnetic field. This pulls the cone back in.

This causes the pressure in the air to vary, producing vibrations. These vibrations are sound waves.

A vibration of the cone can be produced by repeatedly alternating the direction of the current.

Interacting magnetic fields

1 The motor effect is the motion caused by the interaction between a permanent magnet and what? ....

HT The electric motor

2 Explain how an electric motor works.

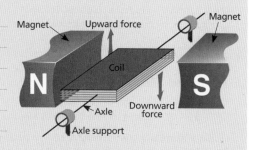

Magnet — Upward force — Magnet
N — Coil — S
Axle — Downward force
Axle support

3 Name **three** household appliances that contain an electric motor. ....

HT Loudspeakers and headphones

4 In headphones, how is variation in the magnetic field produced? ....

5 Add the missing labels to the diagram of a loudspeaker.

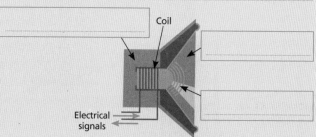

Coil

Electrical signals

6 Explain how an alternating current through a loudspeaker creates sound waves.

7 Induced potential

HT The generator effect

Electromagnetic induction, also called the **generator effect**, uses movement to produce a current. Generators use this effect to produce electricity.

If a wire, or coil of wire, cuts through the lines of force of a magnetic field (or vice versa), a potential difference is induced (produced) between the ends of the wire. If the wire is part of a complete circuit, a current will be induced.

Moving the magnet into the coil induces a current in one direction. A current can be induced in the opposite direction in two ways:

1. Moving the magnet out of the coil.
2. Moving the other pole of the magnet into the coil.

> The same effects work if the magnetic field is stationary and the coil is moved. But remember, if there is no movement of magnet or coil, no current is induced.

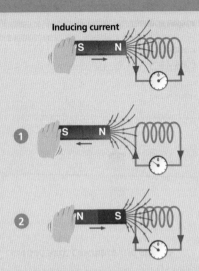

Inducing current

HT Dynamos and moving-coil microphones

A **dynamo** is an electrical generator that produces direct current (dc).

Every half turn, a split ring commutator changes the coil connections. The connections are reversed as the induced potential is about to reverse. The result of this is that the current always flows in the same direction.

Dynamos can be used to power the lights of a bicycle as the wheels turn. The wheel of the dynamo rubs against the tyre, causing a magnet to turn.

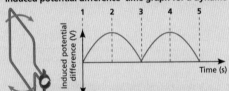

Induced potential difference–time graph for a dynamo

No potential difference is induced when the coil is at 0° (position 1), 180° (position 3) and 360° (position 5, after one full rotation) because it is parallel to the direction of the magnetic field.

Maximum potential difference is induced when the coil is at 90° (position 2) and 270° (position 4) because it is at right angles to the direction of the magnetic field.

Microphones also use the generator effect. Pressure variations in sound waves induce a changing electrical current.

> The diaphragm vibrates as a result of pressure variations in sound waves.
>
> These vibrations cause the coil to vibrate.
>
> A potential difference is induced as the coil moves relative to the magnetic field around the permanent magnet.
>
> A current flows as a result of the induced potential difference.
>
> The induced current changes size and direction, matching the vibrations of the coil.
>
> Electrical signals are generated from these vibrations.

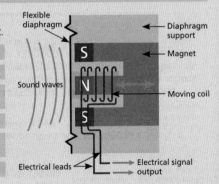

(7) Induced potential

HT The generator effect

1 What is meant by the 'generator effect'?

2 Moving a magnet into a coil of wire induces a current in one direction.

State **two** ways in which a current can be induced in the opposite direction.

HT Dynamos and moving-coil microphones

3 Current always flows in one direction in a dynamo. Explain why.

4 Sketch an induced potential difference–time graph for a dynamo.

5 Explain how a moving-coil microphone uses the generator effect to produce electrical signals from variations in sound waves.

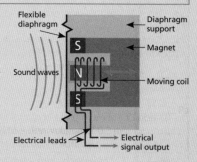

Flexible diaphragm

Diaphragm support

Magnet

S

N

S

Sound waves

Moving coil

Electrical leads

Electrical signal output

Transformers

Transformers: step-up and step-down

A **transformer** changes electrical energy from one potential difference to another potential difference.

An alternating potential difference across the primary coil causes an alternating current to flow (input). This alternating current creates a continually changing magnetic field in the iron core, which creates an alternating potential difference across the ends of the secondary coil (output).

> Transformers have a primary coil and a secondary coil wrapped around a soft iron core.

Step-up and **step-down** transformers are used in the National Grid to ensure the efficient transmission of electricity.

National Grid Process

Step-up transformer

A step-up transformer has more turns in the secondary coil than the primary coil. The potential difference leaving the secondary coil is greater than that across the primary coil.

Step-down transformer

A step-down transformer has fewer turns in the secondary coil than the primary coil. The potential difference leaving the secondary coil is less than that across the primary coil.

Calculating potential difference in transformers

You can calculate the size of the potential difference across the primary and secondary coils:

$$\frac{\text{Potential difference (V)} \text{ across primary coil, } V_p}{\text{Potential difference (V)} \text{ across secondary coil, } V_s} = \frac{\text{Number of turns} \text{ on primary coil, } N_p}{\text{Number of turns} \text{ on secondary coil, } N_s}$$

You can also calculate the size of the potential difference in each coil:

$$V_p I_p = V_s I_s$$

where

V_p is the potential difference in the primary coil and V_s is the potential difference in the secondary coil, in volts (V)
I_p is the current in the primary coil and I_s is the current in the secondary coil, in amperes (A)

a) A transformer has 200 turns on the primary coil and 800 turns on the secondary coil. If a potential difference of 230 V is applied to the primary coil, what is the potential difference across the secondary coil?

$$\frac{V_p}{V_s} = \frac{N_p}{N_s}$$

$$\frac{230\,\text{V}}{V_s} = \frac{200}{800}$$

Substitute the given values into the equation and then solve to work out the potential difference across the secondary coil.

$$\frac{230 \times 800}{200} = 920 \text{ volts}$$

b) The potential difference in the primary coil of a step-down transformer is 25 000 V. The potential difference in the secondary coil is 230 V and the current in this coil is 15 A.

Calculate the current in the primary coil.

$$V_p I_p = V_s I_s$$

So $I_p = \dfrac{(V_s I_s)}{V_s} = \dfrac{(230 \times 15)}{25\,000}$

$$I_p = 0.14\,\text{A}$$

7 Transformers

HT Transformers: step-up and step-down

1 What is a 'transformer'?

_____

_____

2 Draw a diagram of a transformer and label the core, primary coil and secondary coil.

3 Compare step-up and step-down transformers in terms of potential difference.

_____

_____

_____

_____

4 How does the number of turns on the secondary coil in a step-up transformer compare to the number of turns on the primary coil?

_____

_____

HT Calculating potential difference in transformers

5 A transformer has 50 turns on the primary coil. A potential difference of 230V is applied to the primary coil and a potential difference of 1000V is produced on the secondary coil.

a) How many turns are there on the secondary coil?

_____ turns

b) Is it a **step-up** or a **step-down** transformer? _____

6 The potential difference in the primary coil of a step-down transformer is 400000V. The potential difference in the secondary coil is 230V and the current in this coil is 13A.

Calculate the current in the primary coil. Give your answer in standard form.

_____ A

⑧ Our solar system

The composition of the solar system

Our solar system is part of the Milky Way galaxy.

The solar system consists of one star, the Sun. Orbiting the Sun are eight planets, several dwarf planets and more than 100 moons.

Moons are natural satellites that orbit the planets.

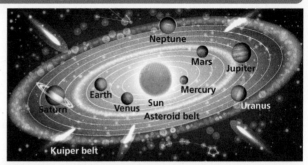

The planets

Planets are large bodies that orbit the Sun.

The **inner planets** are the four planets closest to the Sun. They are Mercury, Venus, Earth and Mars. All of these planets have hard, rocky, solid surfaces.

The **outer planets** are much larger than the inner planets. They are Jupiter, Saturn, Uranus and Neptune. Jupiter and Saturn are known as the 'gas giants'. Uranus and Neptune are also made of gas but have large, icy cores.

The Sun's gravitational field exerts forces on the planets to keep them in their orbits.

The time for light to travel from Neptune to the Earth is about 4 hours.

Earth

The Earth orbits the Sun at a speed of about 30 km/s, or 67 000 mph.

In the diagram, the red arrow represents the force of gravity exerted by the Sun on the Earth. This force keeps the Earth in its orbit.

The distance from the Sun to the Earth is 150 million kilometres. It takes just over 8 minutes for light to travel from the Sun to Earth.

The nearest star to our solar system is Proxima Centauri. It takes light more than 4 years to travel from Proxima Centauri to Earth. Scientists use the distance travelled by light in one year as a unit to measure the huge distances in space. The distance to Proxima Centauri is 4.25 light-years (written as 4.25 ly).

Stars

Formation of stars and planets	Gravitational attraction pulls clouds of dust, rock and gas (nebulae) together.	Heat is created.	The mass eventually becomes hot enough for hydrogen to fuse to form helium, and a star is formed.	This nuclear fusion releases massive amounts of energy and produces all naturally occurring elements.	Smaller masses may also be formed and be attracted by larger masses to become planets.

Stars use hydrogen as their energy source, and they can release energy for millions of years. The Sun is believed to be 5 billion years old and only halfway through its life. It is made up of approximately 74% hydrogen and 24% helium, with traces of heavier elements.

Our Sun is one of many billions of stars in the Milky Way. The stars in a galaxy are often millions of times further apart than the planets in the solar system.

The Milky Way is one of at least a billion galaxies in the universe. Galaxies are often millions of times further apart than the stars within a galaxy.

> The Sun is the star within our solar system. It was formed from a cloud of dust and gas pulled together by gravity.

Not to scale

Our Sun

Our Sun →

Our galaxy the Milky Way

The universe

⑧ Our solar system

The composition of the solar system

1 List the main components of our solar system.

....

....

2 Our solar system is part of which galaxy?

....

The planets

3 What is meant by a 'planet'?

....

4 **a)** Name the **two** 'gas giants' of the solar system.

....

....

b) Name the **two** outer planets of the solar system that are composed of ice and gas.

....

....

5 State the speed, in miles per hour, at which the Earth orbits the Sun.

.... mph

Stars

6 What is the collective term for the dust, rock and gas that were pulled together by gravity to form stars?

....

7 What element is the energy source for stars?

....

8 Approximately how old is the Sun believed to be?

....

8 The life cycle of a star

A star's life

A star remains stable during its life period due to the balance of two forces:

- the force of gravity pulling the star inwards
- huge temperatures (radiation pressure) within the star acting outwards.

> The life cycle of a star depends on its mass.

Towards the end of the star's life, different processes may occur depending on the mass of the star.

Smaller stars

This is the life cycle of stars the size of our Sun after the main sequence stage that our Sun is currently in:

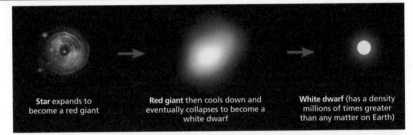

Star expands to become a red giant

Red giant then cools down and eventually collapses to become a white dwarf

White dwarf (has a density millions of times greater than any matter on Earth)

Bigger stars

This is the life cycle of stars at least four times bigger than our Sun after the main sequence stage:

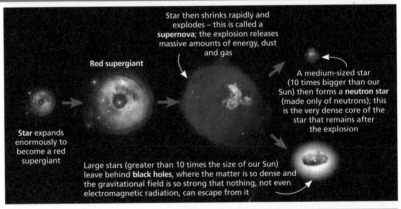

Star expands enormously to become a red supergiant

Red supergiant

Star then shrinks rapidly and explodes – this is called a **supernova**; the explosion releases massive amounts of energy, dust and gas

A medium-sized star (10 times bigger than our Sun) then forms a **neutron star** (made only of neutrons); this is the very dense core of the star that remains after the explosion

Large stars (greater than 10 times the size of our Sun) leave behind **black holes**, where the matter is so dense and the gravitational field is so strong that nothing, not even electromagnetic radiation, can escape from it

Black holes can only be observed indirectly through their effects on their surroundings, e.g. the X-rays emitted when gases from a nearby star spiral into a black hole.

> Larger stars will become red supergiants, before supernovae are formed. From here, either neutron stars or black holes are formed.

Recycling stellar material

Stars need hydrogen as a fuel to undergo nuclear fusion. Helium is produced as a result.

However, during fusion, hydrogen and helium can also fuse together to produce nuclei of heavier elements such as iron.

As a star comes to the end of its life and explodes, its elements are distributed throughout the universe. So, a large variety of different elements are circulated in the universe, not just hydrogen.

These elements can be recycled in the formation of new stars or planets. Atoms of heavier elements are present in the inner planets of the solar system. This leads scientists to believe that the solar system was formed from the material produced when earlier stars exploded.

(8) The life cycle of a star

A star's life

1 Why does a star remain stable during its life period?

Smaller stars

2 At the end of its life, what will the Sun expand to form?

3 Red giants will cool and collapse.
When this happens, what will form?

Bigger stars

4 What is formed when a large star expands?

5 Once a red supergiant has formed, the star then shrinks rapidly and explodes.

What is this called?

6 How is a neutron star formed?

7 What is a black hole?

Recycling stellar material

8 How are the nuclei of heavier elements, such as iron, produced?

8 Orbital motion and satellites

Orbital motion

We have seen that the planets orbit the Sun, and that moons orbit planets. Gravity provides the force to keep these objects in orbit.

Objects go into orbit at speeds of 7600 m/s

Objects leave the Earth's orbit at speeds of 11 200 m/s or more

Objects fall back to Earth at speeds less than 7600 m/s

For an orbit to be stable, the object must be travelling at the correct speed: too fast and it will leave the orbit; too slow and it will fall to the centre of the orbit. The speed of a satellite to remain in orbit varies according to its height. Satellites in geostationary orbit have a speed of around 3000 m/s. The ISS has a lower orbit and a speed of around 7600 m/s.

Orbital speed

When an object moves in a circle at a constant speed, its velocity is changing. This is because its direction is constantly changing.

> Remember that velocity is a vector quantity, so has magnitude and direction.

Since acceleration is the rate of change of velocity, the object moving in a circle is also accelerating, even when travelling at a constant speed.

From Newton's second law, we know that an object will accelerate if acted on by a resultant force. In circular motion, this is centripetal force, acting towards the centre of the circle. Gravity provides the centripetal force that is required to keep the planets and satellites in orbit.

This gravitational attraction between two objects (e.g. a planet and an orbiting moon) decreases with distance. This means that the closer the objects, the greater the force of attraction between them.

If the force increases, so does the acceleration, which means that objects in small orbits travel faster than those in larger orbits, since a greater acceleration means a greater change in velocity.

> When objects are travelling at constant speed in a circular motion, their velocity changes.

Whilst the speed of the pods on the London Eye is constant, there is an acceleration as the direction of the pods is constantly changing as they move around the centre point

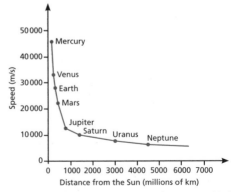

Planets closer to the Sun have a much greater orbital speed than those that are further away

8 Orbital motion and satellites

Orbital motion

1 Name the force that keeps the planets and other satellites in orbit.

....

Orbital speed

2 Explain the difference between speed and velocity.

....

....

....

3 Explain why an object in circular motion at constant speed has a changing velocity.

....

....

....

....

4 Name the resultant force in circular motion.

....

5 Which pair of objects below has a greater force of attraction between them? Explain your answer.

The Sun and the Earth	The Sun and Neptune

....

....

....

....

6 State the relationship between the orbital speed of the planets and their distance from the Sun.

....

....

8 Red-shift

Red-shift

If a wave source is moving away from, or towards, an observer, there will be a change in the:
- observed **wavelength**
- observed **frequency**.

If a light source moves away from us, the wavelengths of the light in its spectrum are longer than if it wasn't moving.

This is known as **red-shift**; the wavelengths 'shift' towards the red end of the electromagnetic spectrum.

There is a red-shift in light observed from most distant galaxies. This means that they are moving away from us very quickly.

This effect is exaggerated in galaxies that are further away. This means that the further away a galaxy is, the faster it's moving away from us.

This observed red-shift suggests that:
- the whole universe is **expanding**
- the universe might have started billions of years ago, from one small place, with a huge explosion know as the '**Big Bang**'.

> Red-shift is the observed increase in wavelength of light from distant objects.

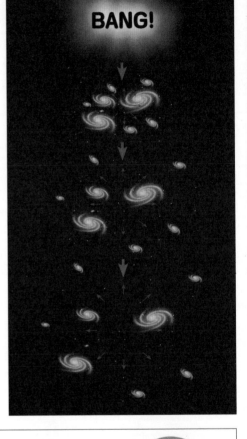

BANG!

To model red-shift, you can draw a wave on a balloon that is not inflated.

When the balloon is inflated, the length of the wave drawn on the balloon increases. This is the same effect as red-shift: the further away the galaxies are, the greater the increase in observed wavelength.

Un-inflated balloon

Inflated balloon

(8) Red-shift

Red-shift

1 Which has a longer wavelength, red or blue light?

....

2 Define the term 'red-shift'.

....

....

....

3 State the relationship between the distance of a galaxy from Earth and red-shift.

....

....

4 State the relationship between the speed of a galaxy moving away from the Earth and red-shift.

....

....

5 When light is red-shifted, its wavelength increases.

What happens to the frequency of red-shifted light?

....

6 Which **two** theories does red-shift provide evidence for?

....

....

7 Light from a distant galaxy is observed to be shifted towards the blue end of the spectrum.

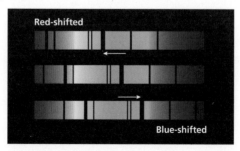

What can be concluded from this observation?

....

....

....

....

Mixed questions (paper 1)

1 A golfer strikes a golf ball and it travels at a speed of 90 m/s. It gains 203 J of kinetic energy.

Calculate the mass of the golf ball in grams.

.... g

2 An apple is hanging from a tree at a height of 2.5 m. The mass of the apple is 250 g.

Taking the gravitational field strength to be 9.8 N/kg, calculate the gravitational potential energy of the apple. Give your answer to 2 significant figures.

.... J

3 An electric hairdryer is connected to the mains supply and has a resistance of 100 Ω. The current flowing through the hairdryer is 5 A.

Calculate the power of the hairdryer.

.... W

4 Hydroelectricity is a renewable energy resource that uses the flow of moving water to generate electricity.

Give **two advantages** and **two disadvantages** of using hydroelectric as an energy resource.

Advantages: ....

....

Disadvantages: ....

....

5 A motor runs for 15 minutes and transfers 4500 C of charge.

Calculate the electrical current flowing through the motor.

.... A

6 A student needs to charge their camera. They connect the camera charger to the mains power supply, with a potential difference of 230 V.

If the charging current is 0.1 A, calculate the resistance in the circuit as the camera charges.

.... Ω

Mixed questions (paper 1)

7 Draw **one** line from each component to the correct current–potential difference graph.

Resistor	Filament lamp	Diode

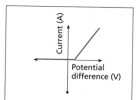 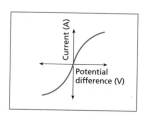 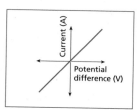

8 A 900 W microwave oven transfers 135 kJ of energy when it is turned on.

For how long is the microwave oven turned on? Give your answer in seconds.

.... s

9 Explain how static charge is used to paint cars and other vehicles.

....

....

....

....

....

....

10 Draw a diagram showing the electric field around a positively charged object.

Mixed questions (paper 1)

11 Balance the nuclear equation.

$$_{53}^{}I \rightarrow _{}^{131}Xe + _{-1}^{}e$$

12 450 kJ of energy are supplied to a 2.0 kg brick. Brick has a specific heat capacity of 840 J/kg°C.

Calculate the change in temperature of the brick. Give your answer to 2 significant figures.

 .... °C

13 0.05 m³ of gas is in a syringe at a pressure of 50 000 Pa. The pressure in the syringe is reduced to 25 000 Pa.

Calculate the new volume of the gas.

.... m³

14 These are the three known isotopes of oxygen: $_{8}^{16}O$ $_{8}^{17}O$ $_{8}^{18}O$

Give **one similarity** and **one difference** between the isotopes by referring to their numbers of protons, neutrons and electrons.

Similarity: ....

....

Difference: ....

....

15 A clay brick has a density of 1800 kg/m³. The dimensions of the clay brick are 23 cm × 11 cm × 8 cm.

Calculate the mass of the brick in kilograms.

.... kg

16 A radioactive isotope has a half-life of 15 minutes.

Assuming that there were 1000 nuclei in the sample at the start, how many nuclei remain after $1\frac{1}{2}$ hours?

.... nuclei

Mixed questions (paper 2)

1 An astronaut has a mass of 70 kg. On the Moon, their weight is 112 N.

Calculate the gravitational field strength on the Moon.

.... N/kg

2 A gardener pushes a wheelbarrow with a force of 50 N. 0.5 kJ of energy is transferred.

How far does the wheelbarrow move?

.... m

3 Red light travels at a speed of 3×10^8 m/s with a frequency of 4×10^{14} Hz.

Calculate the wavelength of red light in metres. Give your answer in standard form.

.... m

4 A gear with a radius of 0.4 m is turned by a smaller gear with a radius of 0.02 m. The moment of the smaller gear is 20 Nm.

Calculate the moment of the larger gear.

.... Nm

5 A student makes a journey of 15.5 km in a time of 30 minutes.

Calculate their average speed, in metres per second. Give your answer to 2 significant figures.

.... m/s

6 An object accelerates at a rate of 2 m/s² to a final velocity of 10 m/s in a time of 3 seconds.

Calculate the initial velocity of the object.

.... m/s

Mixed questions (paper 2)

7 A tractor has a mass of 2500 kg and a momentum of 11 250 kg m/s.

Calculate the velocity of the tractor.

.... m/s

8 40 J of elastic potential energy is stored in a stretched spring, with a spring constant of 4.5 N/m.

Calculate the extension of the spring. Give your answer to 2 significant figures.

.... m

9 A sonar transmitter on a boat sends an ultrasound signal towards the sea bed. 0.8 seconds later, the pulse is detected on the boat. The speed of a sound wave in water is 1500 m/s.

Calculate the depth of the sea.

.... m

10 Three uses of electromagnetic radiation are listed below. For each one, state the type of electromagnetic wave that is used for the given application.

a) Transmitting television signals ....

b) Satellite communications ....

c) Remote controls for televisions ....

11 A diagram of an arrow with a height of 5.5 cm is examined under a lens. The image produced by the lens has a height of 44 cm.

Calculate the magnification of the lens.

....

12 In which direction do magnetic field lines always point? ....

13 Electromagnets are made from a coil of wire. An iron core is often added.

Why is the iron core added?

....

....

Soft iron core | Turns of insulated copper wire

N .... S

14 Explain how red-shift is used as evidence that the universe is expanding.

....

....

....

....

15 The generator effect uses the movement of a magnet relative to a coil of wire to produce a current in the wire. Moving the magnet into the coil induces a current in one direction.

State **one** way in which the direction of the current could be reversed.

....

....

16 A transformer has 100 turns on the primary coil. A potential difference of 230V is applied to the primary coil and a potential difference of 4500V is produced on the secondary coil.

a) How many turns are there on the secondary coil?

.... turns

b) Is the transformer a **step-up** or a **step-down** transformer? Give a reason for your answer.

....

....

17 In the main sequence of its life cycle, a star is in equilibrium owing to the balance of two forces. Describe these forces.

....

....

....

18 Explain why, in order for an orbit to be stable, the object must be travelling at the correct speed.

....

....

19 A current of 13A flows through a 0.5m long wire when it is placed in a magnetic field of flux density 0.75T.

Calculate the force on the wire. Give your answer to 2 significant figures.

.... N

Required practical 1

Determining specific heat capacity

Aim: To determine the specific heat capacity of a substance.

REQUIRED PRACTICAL	
Investigate the specific heat capacity of materials, linking the decrease of one energy store (or work done) to the increase in temperature and subsequent increase in thermal energy stored.	
Sample method	**Considerations, mistakes and errors**
1. Set up the apparatus as shown. 2. Measure the start temperature. 3. Switch on the electric heater for 1 min. 4. Measure the end temperature. 5. Measure the voltage and current to find the power. 6. Repeat for different liquids. 7. Calculate the specific heat capacity. 8. Compare your results to another group's results. If they get similar answers the experiment is **reproducible**.	• The energy provided by the heater is calculated as power × time. However, it could also be found using a joulemeter. • The specific heat capacity is calculated from the energy provided, the mass of the liquid and the temperature change. • If the temperature rise is too high, energy loss to the surroundings will affect the results.
Variables	**Hazards and risks**
• The independent variable is the type of liquid. • The dependent variable is the temperature. • Control variables are the volume of liquid used and energy provided.	• The electric heater could be very hot so you must not touch it directly. • If the liquids become hot they could boil and spit, so safety goggles must be worn and the heater should not be left on for longer than is necessary. • The liquid can be very hot so you must not touch it.

Key points:
- The beaker should be placed on a heat-proof mat to minimise heat loss to the environment.
- The energy transferred can be calculated using the equation $E = Pt$, where P is the power of the heater, measured in watts (W), and t is the time, measured in seconds (s).
- The power of the heater can be determined using the equation $P = IV$, where I is the current, measured in amps (A), and V is the potential difference, measured in volts (V).
- A graph of energy transferred against temperature will give a gradient that is equal to mass × specific heat capacity.

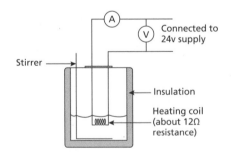

Expected results:
The specific heat capacity of the substance can be compared to data book values. The measured value is likely to be slightly higher due to heat loss to the surroundings.

Required practical 2

Thermal insulators

Aim: To investigate the effectiveness of different materials as thermal insulators.

REQUIRED PRACTICAL	
Investigate the effectiveness of different materials as thermal insulators.	
Sample method	**Considerations, mistakes and errors**
A simple method is to compare different methods of insulation: 1. Take three beakers and wrap each one in a different type of insulation. 2. Fill each beaker with an equal volume of hot water and measure the start temperature of each one. 3. Start the stopwatch and record the temperature every minute for 10 minutes. 4. Plot the results on a graph of time against temperature.	• Time and temperature are examples of continuous data, so a line graph should be used. This will allow any patterns and anomalous results to be easily spotted. • A cooling curve should be a smooth, curved line. If the temperature goes up or down suddenly, this will not fit the pattern of the curve and should be ignored as an anomalous result.
Variables	**Hazards and risks**
• The independent variable is the type of insulation. • The dependent variable is temperature. • The control variables are the volume of water in each beaker and the thickness of insulating material.	• The main hazard is the hot water, which scalds, so care must be taken when pouring the water into the test tubes. • If water is spilt on the insulating material it will affect the results. • The beakers may still be hot even after 10 minutes, so these should be allowed to cool before disposal.

Key points:

• The beakers should be placed on a heat-proof mat to minimise heat loss to the environment.
• A lid could be used to minimise heat loss to the environment.
• When measuring the volume of water using a measuring cylinder, ensure that the measuring cylinder is placed on the table and that you read the water level at eye level.

Expected results:

The material that is the most effective insulator will see the smallest drop in the temperature of the water over the time of the investigation.

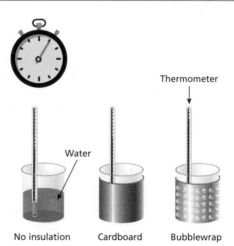

Thermometer

Water

No insulation · Cardboard · Bubblewrap

Required practical 3

Factors affecting resistance

Aim: To investigate the factors that affect the resistance of a piece of wire.

REQUIRED PRACTICAL	
Investigate the factors that affect the resistance of an electrical component.	
Sample method	**Considerations, mistakes and errors**
This example looks at how length affects the resistance of a wire: 1. Set up the standard test circuit as shown. 2. Pre-test the circuit and adjust the supply voltage to ensure that there is a measurable difference in readings taken at the shortest and longest lengths. 3. Use the variable resistor to keep the current through the wire the same at each length. 4. Record the voltage and current at a range of lengths, using crocodile clips to grip the wire at different points. 5. Use the voltage and current measurements to calculate the resistance.	• Adjusting the supply voltage to ensure as wide a range of results as possible is important, as measurements could be limited by the precision of the measuring equipment. • The range of measurements to be tested should always include at least five measurements at reasonable intervals. This allows for patterns to be seen without missing what happens in between, but also without taking large numbers of unnecessary measurements.
Variables	**Hazards and risks**
• The independent variable is the length of the wire. • The dependent variable is the voltage. • The control variable is the current (which is kept the same, because if it was too high it would cause the wire to get hot and change its resistance).	• Current flowing through the wire can cause it to get very hot. • To avoid being burned by the wire: – a low supply voltage should be used, such as the cell in the diagram – adjust the variable resistor to keep the current low.

Key points:
- The potential difference of the power supply should be kept constant during the investigation.
- The temperature of the wire needs to be maintained at a constant temperature during the investigation. In order to do this, disconnect the wire from the circuit between readings and allow it to cool down.
- As the wire gets shorter, the temperature of the wire will increase quickly, so take the reading as soon as the wire is connected to the circuit and then disconnect it.

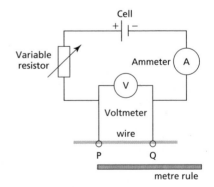

Expected results:

The resistance of the wire should be found to be directly proportional to the resistance, so a graph of resistance against length should produce a straight line that passes through the origin.

Required practical 4

Current-potential difference characteristics

Aim: To investigate the *I–V* characteristics of a filament lamp, diode and resistor at constant temperature.

REQUIRED PRACTICAL	
Investigate the *V–I* characteristics of a filament lamp, a diode and a resistor at constant temperature.	
Sample method	**Considerations, mistakes and errors**
1. Set up the standard test circuit as shown. 2. Use the variable resistor to adjust the potential difference to the lowest setting across the test component. 3. Measure the voltage and current for a range of voltage values. 4. Repeat the experiment at least three times to be able to calculate a mean. 5. Repeat for the other components to be tested.	• Before taking measurements, check the voltage and current with the supply turned off. This will allow zero errors to be identified. • A common error is simply reading the supply voltage as the voltage across the component. At low component resistances, the wires will take a sizeable share of this voltage, resulting in a lower voltage across the component. This is why a voltmeter is used to measure the voltage across the component.
Variables	**Hazards and risks**
• The independent variable is the potential difference across the component (set by the variable resistor) and measured by the voltmeter. • The dependent variable is the current through the component, measured by the ammeter.	• The main risk is that the filament lamp will get hotter as the current increases and could cause burns. If it overheats, the bulb will 'blow' and must be allowed to cool down before attempting to unscrew and replace it.

Key points:

• The temperature of the component needs to be maintained at a constant temperature during the investigation. In order to do this, disconnect the component from the circuit between readings and allow it to cool down.

• In order to take readings for the current flowing in the opposite direction, connect the power supply the other way around.

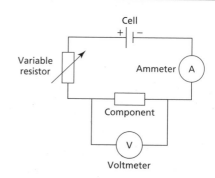

Expected results:

Resistor:

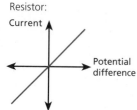

Filament lamp:

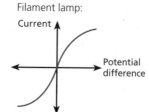

Diode:

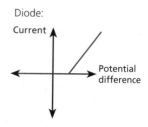

Required practical 5

Determining densities

Aim: To make and record measurements needed to determine the densities of regular and irregular solid objects and liquids.

REQUIRED PRACTICAL	
Investigate the density of regular solids and irregular solids and liquids.	
Sample method	**Considerations, mistakes and errors**
1. Set the equipment up as shown to determine the density of an irregular solid. 2. Record the height of the water in the measuring cylinder and the mass of the solid being tested. 3. Add the solid being tested to the measuring cylinder. 4. Record the new height of the water in the measuring cylinder. 5. Subtracting the original height from the new height gives the volume of the solid being tested. 6. Now the density can be calculated of the solid.	• If a solid that is less dense than water is tested, the volume measurement will be incorrect because the solid will not be fully submerged. • When reading from the measuring cylinder, the reading should be taken from the bottom of the **meniscus**. • The temperature of the water must be exactly the same throughout all tests, as an increase in temperature could cause the material or water to change volume slightly through expansion.
Variables	**Hazards and risks**
• The independent variable is the material being tested. • The dependent variables are the volume and mass. • The control variable is the temperature of the water.	• There are very few hazards, unless the materials being tested are hazardous or react with water. • The main hazard could be a slip hazard if water is spilt.

Key points:
- When reading the scale on the measuring cylinder, ensure that the measuring cylinder is on a flat surface and that you read the meniscus at eye level.
- Be sure to lower the object into the water carefully so as not to cause splashes that would result in the volume reading less than it should do.

Expected results:
The density of the materials tested can be compared to values from a data book.

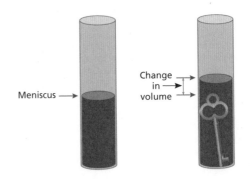

Required practical 6

Force and extension

Aim: To investigate the relationship between force and extension for a spring.

REQUIRED PRACTICAL	
Investigate the relationship between force and extension for a spring.	
Sample method	**Considerations, mistakes and errors**
1. Set up the equipment as shown. 2. Measure the original length of the spring and record this value. 3. Add 100 g (0.98 N) to the mass holder. 4. Measure the extension of the spring and record the result. 5. Repeat steps 2 to 4 for a range of masses from 100 g to 1000 g.	• The extension is the total increase in length from the original unloaded length. It is *not* the total length or the increase each time. • Adding too many masses can stretch the spring too far, which means repeat measurements cannot be made.
Variables	**Hazards and risks**
• The independent variable is the one deliberately changed – in this case, the force on the spring. • The dependent variable is the one that is measured – the extension.	• The biggest hazard in this experiment is masses falling onto the experimenter's feet. To minimise this risk, keep masses to the minimum needed for a good range of results.

Key points:
- When reading the scale on the ruler, ensure that you read it at eye level.
- A marker, such as a pin mounted in Plasticine, can be used to determine the level of the bottom of the spring.

Expected results:

The force and extension of the spring should be directly proportional, up to the limit of proportionality. A graph of force against extension should give a straight line that passes through the origin.

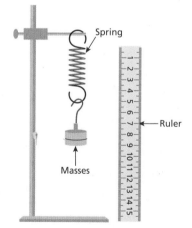

Required practical 7

Acceleration, force and mass

Aim: To investigate the effect of varying the force and/or the mass on the acceleration of an object.

REQUIRED PRACTICAL	
Investigate the effect of varying the force and/or the mass on the acceleration of an object.	
Sample method	**Considerations, mistakes and errors**
1. Set up the equipment as shown with a mass of 100 g. **2.** Release the trolley and use light gates or a stopwatch to take the measurements needed to calculate acceleration. **3.** Move 100 g (0.98 N) from the trolley onto the mass holder. **4.** Repeat steps 2 and 3 until all the masses have been moved from the trolley onto the mass holder. If investigating the mass, keep the force constant by removing a mass from the trolley but not adding it to the holder.	• When changing the force it is important to keep the mass of the system constant. Masses are taken from the trolley to the holder. No extra masses are added. • Fast events often result in timing errors. Repeating results and finding a mean can help reduce the effect of these errors. • If the accelerating force is too low or the mass too high, then frictional effects will cause the results to be inaccurate.
Variables	**Hazards and risks**
• The independent variable is the force or the mass. • The control variable is kept the same. In this case, the force if the mass is changed or the mass if the force is changed.	• The biggest hazard in this experiment is masses falling onto the experimenter's feet. To minimise this risk, masses should be kept to the minimum needed for a good range of results.

Key points:
• Newton's second law states that acceleration is proportional to force, so the greater the force, the greater the acceleration.
• Newton's second law states that acceleration is inversely proportional to mass, so the greater the mass, the smaller the acceleration.

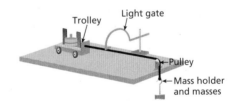

Expected results:
The force and acceleration of the trolley should be directly proportional. A graph of acceleration against force should give a straight line that passes through the origin. The acceleration of the trolley is inversely proportional to the mass, so an acceleration–mass graph will not produce a straight line and so show this inversely proportional relationship.

Required practical 8

Waves in water

Aim: To measure the frequency, wavelength and speed of waves in a ripple tank.

REQUIRED PRACTICAL	
To measure the frequency, wavelength and speed of waves in a ripple tank.	
Sample method	**Considerations, mistakes and errors**
1. Set up the equipment as shown in the diagram. Time how long it takes one wave to travel the length of the tank. Use this to calculate wave speed using: $$speed = \frac{distance}{time}.$$ 2. To find the frequency, count the number of waves passing a fixed point in a second. 3. Estimate the wavelength by using a ruler to measure the peak-to-peak distance as the waves travel. 4. Use a stroboscope to make the same measurements and compare the results. You could also take a picture with a ruler alongside the edge of the tank.	• Using a stroboscope can significantly improve the accuracy of measurements. • By projecting a shadow of the waves onto a screen below the stroboscope, flash speed can be adjusted to make the waves appear stationary. This makes wavelength measurements much more accurate. • For high frequencies that are difficult to count, this equation can be used with the wave speed measurement to calculate the frequency using: $$f = \frac{v}{\lambda}.$$
Variables	**Hazards and risks**
• The key control variable is water depth. It is important to ensure that the depth of the water is kept constant across the tank as, for a given frequency, the depth will affect the speed and wavelength.	• When using a stroboscope there is a risk to people with photo-sensitive epilepsy. It is important to check that there are no at-risk people involved in the experiment or in the area.

Key points:

- To determine the wavelength of the wave, you might find it easier to measure the length of 10 waves and divide this value by 10 (this will particularly help if the wavelength is short).
- The speed of the waves can be determined using the equation:
  speed = wavelength × frequency

Expected results:

For a given speed, waves with a longer wavelength will have a lower frequency.

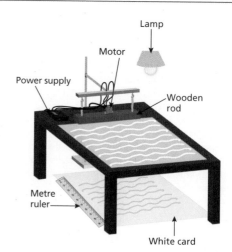

Required practical 9

Reflection and refraction

Aim: To investigate the reflection of light by different types of surface and the refraction of light by different substances.

REQUIRED PRACTICAL	
Investigate reflection and refraction.	
Sample method	**Considerations, mistakes and errors**
1. Set up the equipment as shown. 2. Draw around the semi-circular block. 3. Mark the position of the light ray at the start, at the end, and where it enters and exits the block. 4. Remove the block and connect the marks to show the light rays. 5. Add normal lines and measure the angles of incidence and refraction. 6. Repeat on a new piece of paper for a range of incidence angles.	• It is important to keep the light ray as narrow as possible and the incident at the exact centre of the flat side of the block. If the ray is too wide or off-centre, it can lead to inaccurate measurements. • It is also essential that the block is removed before trying to measure the angles. If the protractor does not line up correctly, it will create a zero error, i.e. the protractor would read a value other than zero, when the angle was zero, making all other readings incorrect.
Variables	**Hazards and risks**
• The independent variable is the angle of incidence. • The dependent variable is the angle of refraction. • The control variable is the material the block is made from.	• If the light box is left on for a long time, the housing close to the bulb can become hot enough to burn. The ray box should be turned off when not in use and care should be taken when moving it.

Key points:
- It is important to keep the ray of light as narrow as possible. Ensure that the slit in the slit card is very fine.
- To improve the accuracy of your results, draw a longer ray and/or use a larger protractor to measure the angles of incidence and refraction.
- To prevent the ray box from getting too hot, turn it off between readings.

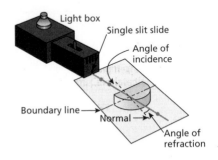

Expected results:

The angle of refraction will be smaller than the angle of incidence as long as the material that the light ray enters from the air is more optically dense than air.

Required practical 10

Infrared radiation

Aim: To investigate how the amount of infrared radiation absorbed or radiated by a surface depends on the nature of that surface.

REQUIRED PRACTICAL	
Investigate how the amount of infrared radiation absorbed or radiated by a surface depends on the nature of that surface.	
Sample method	**Considerations, mistakes and errors**
1. Take four boiling tubes each painted a different colour: matt black, gloss black, white and silver. **2.** Pour hot water into each boiling tube. **3.** Measure and record the start temperature of each tube. **4.** Measure the temperature of each tube every minute for 10 minutes. **5.** The tube that cools fastest emits infrared energy quickest.	• A common error in this experiment is not having the boiling tubes at the same temperature at the start – a hotter tube will cool quicker initially, which can affect results. • Evaporation from the surface of the water can cause cooling too, which will affect the results. To minimise this, block the top of each tube with a bung or a plug of cotton wool.
Variables	**Hazards and risks**
• The independent variable is the colour of the boiling tube. • The dependent variable is the temperature change. • Control variables include volume of water, start temperature and environmental conditions.	• The main hazard is being burned when pouring the hot water and when handling the hot tubes. Using a test tube rack to hold the tubes minimises the need to touch the tubes and means hands can be kept clear when pouring the water into them.

Key points:
- Most of the heat loss from each of the boiling tubes will be due to convection and conduction. The level of conduction and convection will be the same for each boiling tube.
- Any difference in temperature will be due to infrared radiation from the surface.
- Ensure that the same volume of water is added to each of the boiling tubes.

Expected results:

Dark, dull surfaces will be the best emitters of infrared radiation.

Light, shiny surfaces will be the worst emitters of infrared radiation.

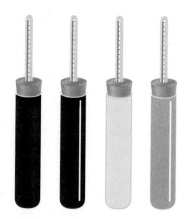

Working scientifically

Physics as the measuring science

Physics is often referred to as the **measuring** science. It is concerned with the behaviour of matter and the interaction of matter.

Just as all chemists use the same chemical symbols, it is important that all physicists use a common language when measuring. This is why all scientists use SI (Système Internationale) units.

SI units

The table below lists the seven base SI units, on which all other units can be based.

Quantity	SI unit
Mass	Kilogram (kg)
Length	Metre (m)
Time	Second (s)
Electric current	Ampere (A)
Temperature	Kelvin (K)
Amount of substance	Mole (mol)
Luminous intensity	Candela (cd)

Interconverting units

We often take measurements using different units to those in the table above, so it is necessary to convert them into SI units before performing any calculations.

For example, we might measure a distance between two towns as 15 km, but if we need to calculate the speed of a vehicle making this journey in metres per second, we have to convert the kilometres into metres.

When converting, we use multiplication factors:
- 1 km = 1000 m, so to convert from kilometres into metres, we multiply by 1000.

So, a distance of 15 km is equal to 15 000 m.

Other useful conversion factors are:
- 1 cm = 0.01 m, so to convert from centimetres into metres, we divide by 100 (or multiply by 10^{-2}).
- 1 mm = 0.001 m, so to convert from millimetres into metres, we divide by 1000 (or multiply by 10^{-3}).
- 1 minute = 60 seconds, so to convert from minutes to seconds, we multiply by 60.
- To convert from degrees Celsius into kelvin, we add 273. So 25°C = 298 K.

Working scientifically

Errors

In any investigations, there may be errors that produce a difference between the collected data and the accurate or true value. Researchers must carefully consider the errors and think about whether this makes the data misleading or if it is valid enough to be used to find a conclusion.

Random errors

A **random error** is an error that changes each time the observation is made. This means:

- they are impossible to predict
- they can cause a large range or spread in the data
- they can produce anomalous results.

Random errors can be due to the researcher using the equipment incorrectly. For example, this could include not reading a scale directly in your eye-line.

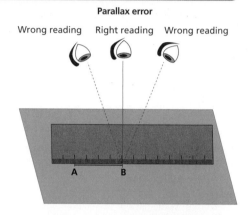

Systematic errors

A **systematic error** is an error that is the same each time the observation is made. This means:

- a measurement will not be close to the true value
- they are possible to correct in the data.

Systematic errors are often due to the equipment not being **calibrated** correctly. For example, this could include a zero error (see below), when you use a balance without first setting it to zero, so it measures a mass as heavier or lighter than it actually is.

Zero errors

A zero error is an error that is caused by a measuring device giving a false reading when the true value of the measured quantity is zero.

For example, if a top pan balance gives a reading when nothing is placed on the balance, this is a zero error.

Zero errors can be managed by subtracting the initial reading from the final reading. For example, if the balance reads 0.5 g before anything is placed on it, and then 10 g of salt are placed on it, the final reading will be 10.5 g. To determine the true measured value, we would subtract 0.5 g from 10.5 g to give a measured value of 10 g.

> There will always be errors in an investigation. But, with careful planning of a method and attention to detail during the practical, they can be minimised. As technology improves and we have more accurate measuring equipment, errors will be reduced.

Working scientifically

Results tables

When carrying out investigations, it is important to record data accurately and in a way that is easy to understand.

Tables are often used as a way of recording experimental data.

Conventions when drawing results tables

To make results tables as easy to understand as possible, these conventions should be followed:
1. Each column in the table should have a heading, including units if appropriate.
2. The data for the independent variable is placed in the first column.
3. The data for the dependent variable is placed in the second column.

Below is an example of a results table that follows these conventions:

Height of ball (m)	Time to fall (s)
0.5	0.2
1.0	0.4
1.5	0.6
2.0	0.8

Notice that there are no units in the body of the table; they are only in the heading for the column.

Repeat readings

The purpose of taking repeat readings during investigations is to identify anomalies (data points that sit outside the pattern of the other data points) and to increase the accuracy of the results.

Repeat readings are recorded in further columns in the results table, with a final column showing the mean. Note that when calculating a mean of the data, any anomalous data points are left out.

Taking the data in the table below, you can see that the anomalous points of 0.9 and 1.3 have been discounted before a mean is calculated.

Height of ball (m)	Time to fall (s) Trial 1	Time to fall (s) Trial 2	Time to fall (s) Trial 3	Mean time to fall (s)
0.5	0.2	0.2	0.9	0.2
1.0	0.4	0.4	0.5	0.4
1.5	0.6	1.3	0.6	0.6
2.0	0.8	0.7	0.6	0.7

Working scientifically

Limitations of scientific knowledge and using evidence

Science is the study of the universe. But, there are limits to scientific knowledge because:
- it may not be possible to design an experiment to test a particular hypothesis
- data cannot be collected as the equipment does not exist – yet!
- the event has already happened and no data was collected.

It is not possible to go back in time and find out how the universe began, for example, or how life on Earth started. So, scientists have to make their best guess about what happened using data that they have collected.

Sometimes, scientists get it wrong, but at the time they do not know. As technology develops, things that were not possible in the past become possible and more data can be gathered, which can be used to develop or disprove previous explanations.

Bias

Bias is when:
- one viewpoint is given, often using persuasive language
- evidence is specially selected
- data is specially collected to support a conclusion
- faulty equipment gives inaccurate results.

Bias can lead to misleading conclusions and could cause harm. Scientists reduce the likelihood of biased results and conclusions by checking each other's work before it is published. This is called **peer review** and gives confidence to the public that the information is likely to be true.

Ethics

Researchers must consider the **ethics** of their experiments. They must consider the risks and benefits and conclude that it is in humanity's best interests to complete the investigation. They should consider the consequences of their research:

- **personally** – the researcher and subjects
- **socially** – groups of people
- **economically** – costs and financial benefits
- **environmentally** – water, air and land.

Researchers themselves often need to ask other experts like religious leaders, other scientists and the public to decide if the research is suitable to be completed. The research should only take place if the benefits equal or outweigh the risks.

Maths skills

What is a conclusion?

In an **investigation**, **data** is collected. A researcher will look at the data and think about what it shows. They then try to find a **conclusion**.

A good conclusion:
- describes the relationship between the **independent variable** (the variable you choose to change) and the **dependent variable** (the variable you measure in the experiment)
- is clearly structured
- is explained using scientific knowledge
- links back to the question you want to answer in the investigation, and the **hypothesis** (what you think will happen).

Relationships in data

Relationships in numerical data can be described by a **line of best fit** on a graph. **Correlation** happens when changing the independent variable shows a change in the dependent variable. Linear correlation can be shown with a straight line of best fit.

Correlation

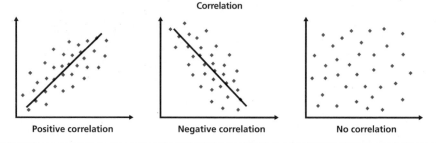

| Positive correlation | Negative correlation | No correlation |

Sometimes there is no correlation in the data, in which case you should not draw a line of best fit. This means there is no relationship between the independent and dependent variables that you have chosen.

The relationship between the independent and dependent variables can be described as **directly proportional** if:
- they produce a straight-line graph, which passes through the origin (0,0)
- the dependent variable doubles when the independent variable has been doubled.

The graph below shows that the extension is directly proportional to the force.

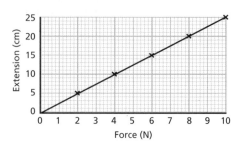

Maths skills

Rearranging equations

During your studies in physics, you will have seen that equations are used to show the relationship between different variables. It is often necessary to rearrange equations in order to calculate an unknown quantity.

The golden rule to follow when rearranging equations is **whatever you do to one side of the equation, you must do to the other**.

Let's take the equation for calculating kinetic energy as an example.

The equation is:

$$E_k = \frac{1}{2}mv^2$$
where
E_k is the kinetic energy, in joules (J)
m is the mass, in kilograms (kg)
v is the speed, in metres per second (m/s)

If the mass is unknown	If the speed is unknown
$E_k = \frac{1}{2}mv^2$	$E_k = \frac{1}{2}mv^2$
Multiply both sides of the equation by 2	Multiply both sides of the equation by 2
$2E_k = mv^2$	$2E_k = mv^2$
Divide both sides of the equation by v^2	Divide both sides of the equation by m
$\frac{2E_k}{v^2} = m$	$\frac{2E_k}{m} = v^2$
	Take the square root of both sides of the equation
	$\sqrt{\frac{2E_k}{m}} = v$

Don't try to carry out more than one step at a time – mistakes can easily be made if you try to complete the rearrangement in one go.

Maths skills

Prefixes

In physics, we often need to deal with either very large or very small numbers. To make this easier, we use **prefixes** before units to indicate a particular multiplication factor.

The prefixes you need to be familiar with are listed in the table below:

Prefix	Multiplication factor
Giga- (G)	1 000 000 000
Mega- (m)	1 000 000
Kilo- (k)	1000
Centi- (c)	$\frac{1}{100}$
Milli- (m)	$\frac{1}{1000}$
Micro- (μ)	$\frac{1}{1000000}$
Nano- (n)	$\frac{1}{1000000000}$

So, a power of 1 megawatt is equal to 1 000 000 W.

Powers of ten

You can see that, when applying the multiplication factors, there are lots of zeros. This can be problematic as it is very easy to add an extra zero, or to leave one out. To overcome this, powers of 10 can be used instead of the multiple zeros.

You can see the powers of ten used for each prefix in the table:

Prefix	Power of ten
Giga- (G)	10^9
Mega- (m)	10^6
Kilo- (k)	10^3
Centi- (c)	10^{-2}
Milli- (m)	10^{-3}
Micro, μ	10^{-6}
Nano- (n)	10^{-9}

So, a wave that has a wavelength of 700 nm has a wavelength of 700×10^{-9} m.

Answers

Page 7

1. Energy cannot be created or destroyed, but can be transferred from one store to another.

2. a) The pear's gravitational potential energy store

   b) The pear's kinetic energy store

3. a) The bicycle's kinetic energy store

   b) Thermal energy store of the brakes

4. *From the left:* chemical; circuit; electric current

5. The kinetic energy of the ball reduces to zero as it is transferred to the thermal energy of the ball and the wall. There is also an energy transfer by waves, as a sound can be heard when the ball makes contact with the wall.

Page 9

1. mass of the object; speed of the object

2. The bus will have greater kinetic energy. This is because they are both moving at the same speed, but the bus has a greater mass. As kinetic energy depends on mass and speed, if the speed is equal, the object with the greater mass will have greater kinetic energy.

3. $E_k = \frac{1}{2} \times 100 \times 7^2 = 2450\,J$ (joules)

4. $E_k = \frac{1}{2} \times 30\,000 \times 56^2$

   $E_k = 47\,040\,000\,J = 47\,040\,kJ$

5. $\frac{2E_k}{v^2} = m$

   $m = \frac{(2 \times 640)}{4^2} = 80\,kg$

6. $\sqrt{\frac{2E_k}{m}} = v$

   $v = \sqrt{\frac{(2 \times 5\,750\,000\,000)}{184\,000}} = 250\,m/s$

Page 11

1. the spring constant; the extension of the spring

2. $E_e = \frac{1}{2} \times 300 \times 0.05^2 = 0.375\,J$

3. Extension = $25\,cm - 5\,cm = 20\,cm$

   Extension = $0.2\,m$

   $E_e = \frac{1}{2} \times 500 \times 0.2^2 = 10\,J$

4. $20 = \frac{1}{2} \times k \times 0.40^2$

   $k = 250\,N/m$

5. mass; gravitational field strength; height

6. $E_p = 0.75 \times 10 \times 1.2 = 9\,J$

7. $E_p = 0.045 \times 10 \times 20 = 9\,J$

8. $637.5\,kJ = 637\,500\,J$

   $637\,500 = 75 \times 10 \times h$

   $h = 850\,m$

Page 13

1. The energy required to raise the temperature of 1 kg of a substance by 1°C.

2. mass; specific heat capacity; change in temperature

3. $\Delta E = 0.0035 \times 385 \times 30$

   $\Delta E = 40.4\,J$ (to 3 s.f.)

4. $\Delta E = 2 \times 4200 \times 82 = 688\,800\,J$

   $\Delta E = 688.8\,kJ$

5. $\frac{\Delta E}{(c\Delta\theta)} = m$

   $m = \frac{78\,750}{(900 \times 35)} = 2.5\,kg$

6. $\frac{\Delta E}{(mc)} = \Delta\theta$

   $\Delta\theta = \frac{28\,350}{(1.5 \times 420)} = 45°C$

Page 15

1. joule; second; watt

2. Motor A is more powerful as it transfers the same energy as Motor B in a shorter time.

3. a) Power = $\frac{10\,000\,000}{(20 \times 60)} = 8333\,W$

   b) $\frac{8333}{1000} = 8.3\,kW$

4. a) The kettle transfers 2500 joules of energy every second.

   b) Power = $\frac{energy}{time}$ so energy = power × time

   Energy = $2500 \times (3 \times 60)$

   Energy = $450\,000\,J = 450\,kJ$

5. a) $2\,MW = 2 \times 10^6\,W$

   b) Energy = $(2 \times 10^6) \times (30 \times 60)$

   Energy = $3\,600\,000\,000\,J = 3600\,MJ$

Page 17

1. Energy cannot be created or destroyed. It can only be transferred from one store to another.

2. Useful – *Any one of:* electrical to light; electrical to sound

   Wasted – electrical to thermal

3. Oiling reduces the friction between two surfaces, which reduces the unwanted energy transfer into the thermal store.

4. *Any two of:* cavity wall insulation; loft insulation; double-glazing; draught excluders; curtains; carpets; turn off appliances when they are not in use

5. It is made of a material with a low thermal conductivity to minimise the rate of thermal energy transfer through the material. This makes it effective as an insulator.

Page 19

1. Efficiency is how much of the energy transferred by a device is transferred as a useful output. The higher the efficiency, the greater the useful energy transfer.

2. An efficiency of greater than 1 would mean that the device was usefully transferring more energy than was inputted into it. This would break the law of conservation of energy.

3. Efficiency = $\frac{6}{15}$ = 0.4

4. Efficiency = $\frac{240}{300}$ = 0.8

5. Total input energy transfer = $\frac{5500}{0.80}$ = 6875 J

6. By wrapping the kettle in insulation

Page 21

1. *Any three from:* fossil fuels (coal, oil and natural gas); nuclear fuel; biofuel; wind; hydroelectric; geothermal; tides; the Sun; water waves

2. *Any two from:* transport; generating electricity; heating

3. Coal; oil; (natural) gas

4. Non-renewable energy resources are those that cannot be replaced within a lifetime and will eventually run out.

5. Advantage: *Any one from:* coal is relatively cheap and easy to obtain; coal-fired power stations can be set up relatively quickly

Disadvantage: *Any one from:* burning coal produces carbon dioxide, a greenhouse gas; burning coal produces more carbon dioxide per unit of energy than oil or gas does; burning coal produces sulfur dioxide, which causes acid rain and is costly to remove from the process

6. A renewable energy resource is one that can be replenished as it is used. Examples include: biofuel; wind; hydroelectric; geothermal; tides; Sun; water waves

7. Advantage: *Any one from:* no fuel and little maintenance required for wind turbines; turbines can be built offshore; no pollutant gases produced

Disadvantage: *Any one from:* wind turbines can cause noise and visual pollution; wind is not very flexible in meeting energy demand; large capital outlay

Page 23

1. A complete path around which an electric current can flow.

2. A cell or a battery of cells

At least one device that can transfer energy, e.g. a lamp

Wires, called connecting leads, which join the cell to the components in the circuit

A switch is usually included

3. a)   **b)**

c)   **d)**

4.

5.

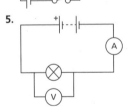

Page 25

1. The rate of flow of electric charge

2. Charge = current × time

3. $Q = 3 \times 600 = 1800$ C

4. $Q = 15 \times 480 = 7200$ C

5. $t = \frac{2000}{1.5} = 1333.3$ s

6. $I = \frac{1200}{900} = 1.3$ A

Page 27

1. The electric current will increase.

2. Potential difference = current × resistance

3. $V = 0.005 \times 300 = 1.5\,V$

4. $V = 3.0 \times 250 = 750\,V$

5. $I = \frac{12}{4} = 3\,A$

6. $R = \frac{400}{10} = 40\,\Omega$

Page 29

1. Resistance is a measure of how hard it is to get a current through a component at a particular potential difference. Potential difference = current × resistance

2. If the values are directly proportional to one another, when plotted on a graph they will form a straight line with a positive gradient that passes through the origin.

3. a) a length of wire

b) *Any one from:* LDR; thermistor; filament lamp; diode

4.

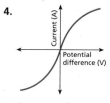

5. a)

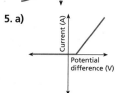

b) The curve is this shape because no current flows through the diode in the reverse direction, making the resistance very high. Current only flows in one direction.

6. a) *Any suitable use, e.g.* thermostats in heating systems

b) *Any suitable use, e.g.* switching lights on when it gets dark

Page 31

1. They are connected in one single loop.

2. 0.3 A

3. As potential difference is shared between components, the value of the potential difference across each bulb will be $\frac{4.5}{2} = 2.25\,V$

4. They are connected in separate loops.

5. Ammeter X will have the highest reading. This is because the total current in the circuit (measured by ammeter X) is equal to the sum of the currents flowing through the individual components (measured by ammeters Y and Z).

6. *Table completed as follows:*
Series circuit column (from top): same; shared; sum
Parallel circuit (from top): sum; same; less

Page 33

1. An alternating potential difference produces an electric current that regularly changes direction.

2.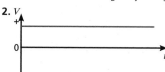

3. Frequency = 50 Hz
Potential difference = 230 V

4. The mains supply is an alternating supply. This allows the electricity to be transmitted more efficiently.

5. Copper is used because it is a good conductor of electricity.

6.

Wire	Function
Live	Carries **alternating** current from the **supply** to the **device**.
Neutral	**Completes** the circuit to allow **current** to flow to the device.
Earth	**Safety** wire; this stops the appliance from becoming **live**.

Page 35

1. Electrical power is a measure of the rate of energy transfer. The greater the power, the faster the rate of energy transfer.

2. $P = 0.7 \times 230 = 161\,W$

3. $P = 8.45^2 \times 35 = 2499\,W$

4. $I = \frac{8000}{250} = 32\,A$

5. $V = \frac{4.5}{3} = 1.5\,V$

6. $R = \frac{2600}{13^2} = 15.4\,\Omega$ (to 3 s.f.)

7. $I = \sqrt{\frac{900}{100}} = 3\,A$

Page 37

1. The power of the appliance.
The time it is switched on for.

2. Energy transferred = power × time

3. $E = 60 \times (20 \times 60) = 72\,000\,J$

4. $t = \frac{180\,000}{1500}$

$t = 120$ seconds = 2 minutes

5. $P = \frac{702\,000}{(3 \times 60 \times 60)} = 65\,W$

6. Energy = charge × potential difference

7. $E = 230 \times 6000 = 1\,380\,000\,J$

8. $Q = \frac{165\,600}{230} = 720\,C$

9. $V = \frac{150}{100} = 1.5\,V$

Page 39

1. C

2. Step-up transformers are used to increase the potential difference so that electricity is transmitted at a high voltage.

3. If electricity is transmitted at a very high voltage, the current will be very low. This reduces the energy loss through heating, making the electricity transmission more efficient.

4. Step-down transformers are used to decrease the potential difference so that electricity can be delivered to consumers at a safe voltage.

5. Cables are very thick to reduce the electrical resistance. This means that less energy will be dissipated as heat, increasing the efficiency of electricity transmission.

Page 41

1. a) Electrons

b) Negatively charged. The comb has gained electrons, which are negatively charged.

c) Electric field

d) A non-contact force

2. a) The rod will gain positive charge because it has lost negatively charged electrons.

b) The force will be repulsive since both rods have a positive charge and like charges repel.

3. a)

Electrostatic paint spray gun

b) The paint droplets are all positively charged so they will repel each other, making the jet from the electrostatic gun much wider.

Page 43

1. An electric field is a region of space within which another charged object would experience a **force**.

2.

3. They show the direction in which a point positive charge would move if placed into the field.

4. The greater the distance from the charged object, the weaker the electric field strength (or vice versa).

5. *Any suitable answer, e.g.* There is a build-up of electrons on a surface. This results in a charge difference between the surface and the earth. Eventually, enough electrons build up to give a large charge difference. Electrons from the charged surface jump to the earth and this is seen as a spark.

Page 45

1. mass and volume

2. Since the volume of a gas is larger than the volume for the same mass as a solid, the density of a gas is less than that of the solid.

Gas	Solid
Low density	High density

3. Density $= \frac{\text{mass}}{\text{volume}}$

Density is measured in kg/m^3

Mass is measured in kg

Volume is measured in m^3

4. $\rho = \frac{1134.3}{0.1} = 11\,343\,kg/m^3$

5. $m = \frac{7.5}{1000} = 7.5 \times 10^{-3}\,kg$

$v = \frac{7.5 \times 10^{-3}}{19\,320}$

$v = 3.88 \times 10^{-7}\,m^3$

6. Since the density of the iron is almost 8 times that of the water, the iron nail will sink in water.

Page 47

1.

2. a) The temperature at which a pure substance changes from a solid to a liquid.

b) The temperature at which a pure substance changes from a liquid to a gas.

3.

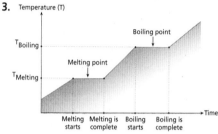

4. Similarity: Both evaporation and boiling are physical changes that involve a liquid turning into a gas.

Difference *(any one from)*: Evaporation happens at any temperature between the melting point and boiling point of a substance, whereas boiling only happens at the boiling point; The energy for evaporation comes mainly from the kinetic energy of the substance, whereas the energy for boiling comes mainly from the surroundings of the substance.

5. The internal energy of a system is the sum of the kinetic and potential energies of all of the particles that make up the system.

Page 49

1. The mass of the substance being heated.
The substance being heated.
The energy input.

2. The energy required to increase the temperature of 1 kg of a substance by 1°C.

3. The substance with the **lower** specific heat capacity will have a greater temperature rise.

4. change in thermal energy = mass × specific heat capacity × change in temperature

5. $\Delta E = (5 \times 10^{-3}) \times 2000 \times 80$

$\Delta E = 800\,J$

6. $c = \frac{146\,250}{(0.25 \times 30)} = 19\,500\,J/kg°C$

7. $m = \frac{101\,500}{(900 \times 205)}$

$m = 0.55\,kg = 550\,g$

Page 51

1. Latent heat is the energy that is added to a substance as it changes state. This is the energy needed to overcome the intermolecular forces.

2. The specific latent heat of fusion is the energy required to melt 1 kg of a substance, whereas the specific latent heat of vaporisation is the energy required to change the state of 1 kg of a substance from liquid to gas.

3. energy = mass × specific latent heat

4. $E = (\frac{20}{1000}) \times 275\,700 = 5514\,J$

5. $L = \frac{1\,995\,000}{5} = 399\,000\,J/kg$

6. $m = \frac{1\,710\,000}{855\,000} = 2\,kg$

Page 53

1. *Any two from:* particles are identical unless they are given different colours; the individual atoms in the particles are not shown; intermolecular forces between particles are not shown

2. The particles in a gas move with a constant, random motion (in random directions) at a range of different speeds.

3. An increase in temperature leads to an increase in the average kinetic energy of the particles.

4. $E_k = \frac{1}{2}mv^2$
As kinetic energy is proportional to the square of the speed, if the kinetic energy doubles, the average speed of the gas particles quadruples.

5. Pressure is caused by collisions between the gas particles and the walls of the container in which it is held.

6. If the temperature is increased, the average kinetic energy of the particles increases. This means that they will collide with the walls of the container more frequently and with more energy. The increasing frequency of collisions raises the pressure of the gas, since each collision creates a force.

Page 55

1. Increasing the volume means that the particles will be further apart. This reduces the number of collisions per second with the walls of the container, reducing the pressure exerted by the gas.

2. doubles

3. $p_2 = \frac{(100000 \times 25)}{50} = 50000\,\text{Pa}$

4. $25000 \times 1000 = 100000 \times V_2$

$V_2 = \frac{(25000 \times 1000)}{100000} = 250\,\text{cm}^3$

5. $p_1 = \frac{(10000 \times 20)}{10} = 20000\,\text{Pa}$

6. $V_1 = \frac{(5.5 \times 10^7) \times 0.3}{2.5 \times 10^7} = 0.66\,\text{m}^3$

Page 57

1.

Atomic particle	Relative mass	Relative charge
Proton	1	+1
Neutron	1	0
Electron	$\frac{1}{2000}$	−1

2. Ratio $= \frac{1.5 \times 10^{-14}}{1.7 \times 10^{-15}} = 8.8$

8.8 times bigger

3. Number of neutrons = 27 − 13

Number of neutrons = 14

4. Number of protons = 12

Number of electrons = 12

Number of neutrons = 12

5. Isotopes are atoms of the same element with the same number of protons, but a different number of neutrons.

6. Similarity: all three isotopes have 1 proton and 1 electron

Difference: protium has no neutrons, deuterium has 1 neutron and tritium has 2 neutrons.

Page 59

1. Atoms were thought to be tiny, solid, indivisible spheres.

2. Electron

3.

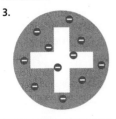

4.

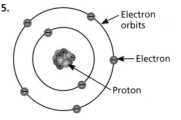

Most alpha particles passed straight through the gold foil	The nucleus is very small and very dense
Some alpha particles were deflected at small angles	Most of the atom is empty space
A very small number of alpha particles were deflected straight back	The nucleus is positively charged

5.

Electron orbits

Electron

Proton

6. James Chadwick

Page 61

1. The nuclei of unstable atoms may disintegrate and emit radiation.

2. It is impossible to tell which nuclei will decay or when a particular nucleus will decay.

3. A helium nucleus (or two protons and two neutrons)

4. An alpha particle contains two protons so when a nucleus emits an alpha particle, the proton number of the remaining nucleus decreases by two. Since the proton number determines the element, a different proton number means a new element has been formed.

5. proton and electron

6. Ionisation can damage or kill healthy cells within the body.

7. The activity is the rate at which unstable nuclei decay. The count rate is the rate at which the decay is detected.

8.

Type of radiation	Penetration power	Range of air	Ionising power
Alpha	Stopped by **skin / a sheet of paper**	< 5 cm	**High**
Beta	Stopped by 2–3 mm of aluminium foil	~ 1 m	Low
Gamma	Stopped by **thick lead / concrete**	> 1 km	**Very low**

Page 63

1. a) $^{4}_{2}\text{He}$ b) $^{0}_{-1}\text{e}$

2. Gamma radiation is in the form of an uncharged electromagnetic wave, which has no mass, and so the emission of a gamma wave does not change the charge or mass of the nucleus.

3. *Table completed as follows:* Decreases by **2**; **Decreases** by 4

4. *Table completed as follows:* Increases by **1**; **Remains unchanged**

5. $X = 235$ $Y = 94$

6. *Missing values are (from the left):* 11; 7; 0

Page 65

1. It is not possible to tell which nuclei in a sample will decay, or when a particular nucleus will decay.

2. *Any one from:* The time taken for the number of nuclei in a sample to halve; The time taken for the activity / count rate of the sample to fall to half of its initial value

3. 5 minutes

4.

Time (days)	Activity (Bq)
0	600
5	300
10	150
15	75
20	37.5
25	18.75
30	9.375

Activity after 30 days will be 9.375 Bq

5. a) $\frac{120}{30} = 4$ half-lives

$(\frac{1}{2})^4 = \frac{1}{16}$

So, $\frac{1}{16}$th will remain after 120 years.

b) $1000 \times (\frac{1}{16}) = 62.5$ g

Page 67

1. *Any suitable similarity and difference, e.g.*
Similarity: Both irradiation and contamination can cause damage to living cells and so must be carefully considered.

Difference: *(any one from)*: Irradiation is the exposure of an object to radiation, whereas contamination is the presence of material containing radioactive atoms on or in the object; If an object is irradiated, this stops as soon as the source is removed and the object does not become radioactive, whereas a contaminated object will remain radioactive for as long as the source is on or in it.

2. The food is exposed to a gamma source. The gamma rays destroy living tissue and therefore kill bacteria on the surface of the food.

3. *Any suitable use, e.g.* sterilising surgical instruments; destroying cancerous tumours

4. A radioactive source could be introduced into the gas supply. The movement of this source could then be tracked. At the site of the leak, large amounts of radiation would be detected.

5. The half-life of the source should be carefully considered. It needs to be long enough for the detection to occur, but short enough that the source is not active for longer than is necessary to detect the leak. For this reason, a source with a half-life of hours, rather than days, should be used.

Page 69

1. *Any three from:* radon gas (from uranium in rocks / soil); gamma rays (from rocks / soil / building materials); food; cosmic rays

2. Sieverts (Sv)

3. A very long half-life means that the source will remain active for an extremely long time. Disposal of nuclear waste needs to be carefully controlled in order to prevent the release of potentially dangerous material into the local environment.

4. The source needs to pass through the skin in order to be detected. Alpha sources are stopped by paper and so would not pass through the skin. It therefore wouldn't be detected. Alpha sources are more ionising and therefore more dangerous to introduce into the body.

5. Advantage: The gamma source can potentially destroy the tumour.

Disadvantage: Healthy cells may be destroyed in the process.

Page 71

1. uranium-235; plutonium-239

2. A neutron

3. Two smaller nuclei; extra neutrons; energy

4.

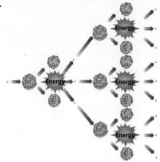

5. Nuclear fusion is the joining together of two or more small nuclei to form a larger nucleus.

6. Hydrogen is converted into helium, providing the energy needed to keep the Sun burning.

Page 73

1. A scalar quantity is a quantity with only magnitude (size)

2. *Any two from:* energy; mass; time; temperature; speed

3. A scalar quantity has only magnitude whereas a vector quantity has magnitude and direction.

4. *Any two from:* force; velocity; momentum; acceleration; displacement

5.

40 N   70 N

The resultant force is 30 N to the right.

6. *Any three from:* friction; air resistance; normal contact force; tension

7. gravitational; electrostatic; magnetic

Page 75

1. The gravitational field strength is the gravitational force on a 1 kg object. It is measured in N/kg.

2.

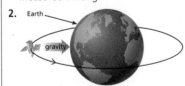

3. Weight is the force of gravity on an object. It is measured in newtons, N.

4. Weight = mass × gravitational field strength

5. $W = 5 \times 10 = 50\,N$

6. $\dfrac{W}{m} = g$

$g = \dfrac{104}{65} = 1.6\ \text{N/kg}$

Page 77

1. Resultant force = 10 − 5

Resultant force = 5 N to the right

2. Resultant force = 7 − 5

Resultant force = 2 N downwards

3.

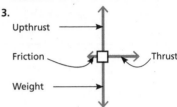

4.

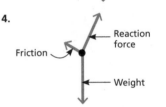

5.

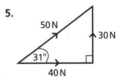

Horizontal component = 40 N

Vertical component = 30 N

Page 79

1. When a force moves an object, work is done.

2. Work done = energy transferred

3. Work done = force × distance. Work done is measured in joules (J), force is measured in newtons (N) and distance is measured in metres (m).

4. $W = 15 \times 2 = 30\,J$

5. $W = Fs$, so $F = \dfrac{W}{s}$

$F = \dfrac{240}{12} = 20\,N$

6. $W = Fs$, so $s = \dfrac{W}{F}$

$F = \dfrac{4500}{1000} = 4.5\,m$

Page 81

1. Extension = 60 − 20 = 40 cm

Extension = 0.4 m

2. Compression = 5 − 1 = 4 cm

3. Force = spring constant × extension

Force is measured in newtons (N); spring constant is measured in newtons per metre (N/m); extension is measured in metres (m)

4. The graph is a straight line that passes through the origin.

5. $E_e = \frac{1}{2}ke^2$

$E_e = \frac{1}{2} \times 32 \times 0.3^2 = 1.44$ J

6. $\sqrt{\frac{2E_e}{k}} = e$

$e = \sqrt{\frac{2 \times 20}{2.5}} = 4$ m

7. $\sqrt{\frac{2E_e}{k}} = e$

$e = \sqrt{\frac{2 \times 15}{50}} = 0.77$ m

Final length = 0.05 + 0.77 = 0.82 m

So 82 cm

Page 83

1. Load   Effort

Fulcrum

2. Increase the distance from the effort force to the fulcrum.

Reduce the distance from load to the fulcrum.

Increase the size of the effort force.

3. Moment = force × distance

Moment is measured in newton metres (Nm); force is measured in newtons (N); distance is measured in metres (m)

4. $M = 7.5 \times 0.3 = 2.25$ Nm

5. $F = \frac{M}{d}$

$F = \frac{11.25}{0.75} = 15$ N

6. $F = \frac{M}{d}$

$F = \frac{150}{0.4} = 375$ N

$M = Fd$

$M = 375 \times 0.1 = 37.5$ Nm

Page 85

1. Pressure $= \frac{\text{force}}{\text{area}}$

Pressure is measured in pascals (Pa); force is measured in newtons (N); area is measured in metres squared (m²) (*Allow* newtons per square metre, N/m²)

2. $P = \frac{1.5}{0.8} = 1.875$ Pa

3. The liquid pushes against the container walls. The weight of liquid pushes down on the liquid below. Liquids cannot be compressed so at deep levels the liquid pushes harder on the container walls.

4. $P = h\rho g$

$P = 0.7 \times 1000 \times 9.8 = 6860$ Pa

5. The air closer to the Earth's surface is squashed by the weight of the atmosphere above. So, the air molecules at sea level are pushed closer together than those at high altitude (e.g. at the top of a mountain).

Page 87

1. Distance is the total number of metres, kilometres or miles travelled, whereas displacement is the distance travelled in a straight line in a given direction from start to finish.

2. Distance travelled and time taken

3. *Any suitable answers, e.g.*

Walking	1.5 m/s
Running	3 m/s
Cycling	6 m/s

4. Distance = speed × time

Distance is measured in metres (m); speed is measured in metres per second (m/s); time is measured in seconds (s)

5. $s = 3.5 \times 1800$

$s = 6300$ m = 6.3 km

6. $v = \frac{s}{t}$

$v = \frac{21600}{3600} = 6$ m/s

7. Velocity is the speed of an object in a given direction. Even if the speed is constant, an object in a circle is constantly changing direction, which means its velocity is also constantly changing.

Page 89

1. Acceleration is the rate of change of velocity. It is measured in metres per second squared (m/s^2).

2. Acceleration = $\dfrac{\text{change in velocity}}{\text{time}}$

3. $a = \dfrac{\Delta v}{t}$

$a = \dfrac{6}{6} = 1\,m/s^2$

4. $a = \dfrac{\Delta v}{t}$

$\Delta v = a \times t$

$\Delta v = 2 \times 15 = 30\,m/s$

5. a) The acceleration of the object

   b) The total distance travelled by the object

6. a)

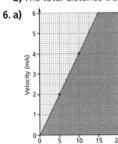

   b) Finding the gradient of the line over the first 15 seconds = $\dfrac{6}{15} = 0.4\,m/s^2$

   c) Calculating the area under the line = $(0.5 \times 15 \times 6) + (5 \times 6) = 75\,m$

Page 91

1. An object will remain stationary or move at a constant speed, in the same direction, unless acted upon by an unbalanced force.

2. The forces of weight and normal reaction force are equal and opposite. This means that there is no resultant force acting on the book. According to Newton's first law, no resultant force means that a stationary object will have zero acceleration.

3. An object will accelerate when acted upon by an unbalanced force.

4. $F = 20\,000 \times 2 = 40\,000\,N$

5. $a = \dfrac{F}{m} = \dfrac{500}{100} = 5\,m/s^2$

6. Newton's third law states that for every action force, there is an equal and opposite reaction force.

7. The pair of forces must:
   - act on different bodies
   - act in opposite directions
   - act along the same line
   - be of the same type (e.g. both gravitational forces)
   - be of the same magnitude.

Page 93

1. 0.2 to 0.9 s

2. a) The distance travelled during the driver's reaction time.

   b) The distance travelled between the driver applying the brakes and the car coming to a stop.

3. 9 + 14 = 23 m

4. *Any three from:* Tiredness – if a driver is tired, their reaction time will increase; Taking drugs – if a driver is taking medication or illegal substances, it may increase reaction time; Drinking alcohol – this also increases reaction time; Distractions, such as using a mobile phone or children playing in the back of a car, will increase reaction time.

5. The speed of the vehicle – greater speed increases the braking distance; The road conditions – wet or icy roads can reduce the friction between the tyres and the road surface, increasing the braking distance; The condition of the vehicle – worn brakes or worn tyres increase the braking distance.

6. The increase in frictional forces between the brakes and the wheels can cause the brakes to overheat.

Page 95

1. Momentum = mass × velocity

2. $p = 80 \times 3 = 240\,kg\,m/s$

3. $v = \dfrac{15\,000}{1500} = 10\,m/s$

4. In a closed system, the momentum before a collision is equal to the momentum after a collision.

5. Cars have crumple zones to increase the time taken for the vehicle's momentum to reduce to zero. An increase in time will result in a decrease in the force experienced by the occupants of the car since force = $\dfrac{\text{change in momentum}}{\text{time}}$

6. a) Force = $\dfrac{(60 \times 10)}{0.2} = 3000\,N$

   b) Force = $\dfrac{(60 \times 10)}{2} = 300\,N$

Page 97

1. a) *One of:* light; water

   b) Sound

2.

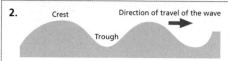

Crest — Direction of travel of the wave

Trough

3. 35°

4. The amplitude of a wave is the maximum displacement of the wave from its undisturbed position.

5. The frequency of a wave is the number of waves passing a given point every second. The unit of frequency is hertz (Hz).

6. $f = \frac{1}{T} = \frac{1}{10}$

$f = 0.1\,\text{Hz}$

7. Wave speed = frequency × wavelength

8. $v = f\lambda = 500 \times 0.001$

$v = 0.5\,\text{m/s}$

9. $v = f\lambda$

So $\lambda = \frac{v}{f}$

$\lambda = \frac{(3 \times 10^6)}{3000} = 1000\,\text{m}$

Page 99

1. 20 Hz to 20 000 Hz

2. Detecting flaws and cracks; pre-natal scanning; cleaning delicate objects

3. As ultrasonic waves pass from one medium or substance into another, they are partially reflected at the boundary. The time taken for these reflections is a measure of how far away the boundary is. This can be used to build up an image of the inside of the human body.

4. P-waves are longitudinal waves and can pass through solids and liquids. S-waves are transverse and so cannot pass through liquids.

5. Since S-waves cannot travel through a liquid, they are not detected on the other side of the Earth. This provides evidence for the existence of a liquid core. The size of the core can be found by looking at where the detection of S-waves begins and ends.

6. Time taken for the pulse to reach the sea bed $= \frac{0.2}{2} = 0.1$ seconds

$s = vt = 1500 \times 0.1$

$s = 150\,\text{m}$

Page 101

1. radio waves, microwaves, infrared, visible, ultraviolet, X-rays, gamma rays

2. Speed $= (7.0 \times 10^{14}) \times (4.3 \times 10^{-7})$

Speed $= 3.0 \times 10^8\,\text{m/s}$

3. Refraction is the change of direction of a wave as it crosses a boundary between two transparent materials.

4. UV radiation; X-rays; gamma rays

5. If radio waves are absorbed, they may create an alternating current with the same frequency of the radio waves.

6. X-rays and gamma rays are both types of ionising radiation. This means that they can cause mutations in cells in the body, which can cause cancer.

Page 103

1.

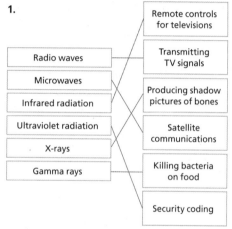

Radio waves — Remote controls for televisions

Radio waves — Transmitting TV signals

Microwaves — Satellite communications

Infrared radiation — Killing bacteria on food

Ultraviolet radiation — Security coding

X-rays — Producing shadow pictures of bones

Gamma rays — Producing shadow pictures of bones

2. The microwaves can be absorbed by water in the cells in the body, which can heat up, causing them to become damaged.

3. X-rays and gamma rays pass through soft tissue (some is absorbed). A high dose of X-rays or gamma rays can kill cells in the body; a low dose can lead to cancerous tumours forming in the body.

4. Ultraviolet (UV) radiation passes through the skin to the tissues below. A high dose of UV radiation can kill body cells; a low dose of UV radiation can lead to cancer.

Page 105

1. a)   **b)**

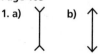

2. The image formed from a diverging lens is virtual and upright.

3.

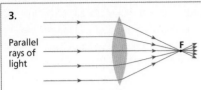

Parallel rays of light   F

4. Magnification $= \frac{10}{2.5} = 4$

5. Magnification $= \frac{\text{image size}}{\text{object size}}$

So object size $= \frac{\text{image size}}{\text{magnification}}$

Ladybird size $= \frac{5}{10} = 0.5\,\text{cm}$

6. In specular reflection, the rays of visible light are reflected from a plane surface and therefore in a regular pattern, producing a clear image. In diffuse scattering, the rays of light are reflected from an uneven surface and therefore in all directions, producing a blurred image.

Page 107

1. The greater the temperature, the greater the amount of infrared radiation emitted in a given time.

2. A perfect black body is an object that absorbs all of the radiation incident on it. It does not transmit or reflect any of the radiation on it.

3. A hot cup of tea cools down because, the hotter the object, the more infrared radiation it emits in a given time. As the radiation is emitted, the temperature of the cup of tea decreases.

4. The rates of emission and absorption of radiation; the reflection of radiation into space.

5. Clouds reflect the infrared radiation emitted from the Earth back to its surface, increasing the temperature. If it is a clear night, there are no clouds, so the radiation emitted is lost to space, reducing the temperature of the Earth.

Page 109

1. North pole; south pole

2. Two bar magnets can be placed close to one another, but not touching. If the two north poles are close, the magnets will repel. If the north pole of one magnet is placed close to the south pole of the second magnet, they will attract each other.

3. A region around a magnet where a force acts on another magnet or magnetic material

4. *Any two from:* nickel; steel; cobalt; neodymium

5. A permanent magnet produces its own magnetic field.
Any suitable example, e.g. iron; cobalt; nickel

6. Repeatedly stroking the nail with the pole of a magnet from head to point magnetises the nail.

7. A material that becomes magnetic when placed in a magnetic field

Page 111

1. A coil of wire with an electric current passing through it. When the current flows, a magnetic field is generated around the coil of wire.

2. A long coil of wire with a soft iron core

3.

Magnet	Type of magnet	Strength of field
Bar magnet	**Permanent**	Quite strong
Electromagnet with air core	Temporary	**Weak**
Solenoid with iron core	**Temporary**	Very strong

4. Electromagnets can be switched on or off by disconnecting the battery.

The current of an electromagnet can be changed, so the strength of the magnetic field can be controlled.

The direction of the current in an electromagnet can be reversed by reversing the battery connections.

5. *Any three from:* loudspeakers; magnetic locks; data storage; headphones; cranes; electric bells

6. Each earpiece in a set of headphones contains a permanent magnet and an electromagnet. The interaction between them causes the vibration that produces sound.

Page 113

1. When a wire (conductor) carrying an electric current is placed in a magnetic field, the magnetic field formed around the wire interacts with the permanent magnetic field and this causes the wire to experience a force, which makes it move.

2. By increasing the size of the current

By using stronger magnets / increasing the strength of the magnetic field

3. By turning the cells around / reversing the direction of flow of current

By reversing the direction of the magnetic field

4. Lining up the first finger with the magnetic field, pointing left to right (from north to south), and the second finger with the current, pointing down (from positive to negative), the thumb will point towards us. Therefore, the wire will move in this direction.

5. Force = magnetic flux density × current × length

6. $F = BIL = 1.5 \times 10 \times 2.5$

$F = 37.5\,N$

Page 115

1. An electromagnet

2. A battery is connected to the coil, which becomes an electromagnet. The coil's magnetic field and the field produced by the magnets interact. The interaction creates an upward force on one side of the coil. The interaction also creates a downward force on the other side of the coil. The upward and downward forces make the coil rotate clockwise.

3. *Any three suitable answers, e.g.* washing machine; tumble dryer; microwave oven; electric tin opener; electric food mixer; electric fan

4. By varying the electric current passing through

5.

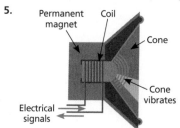

6. The current in the coil of wire produces a magnetic field. This magnetic field interacts with the permanent magnet, creating a force. This causes the cone to move outwards. The direction of the current is reversed. This reverses the direction of the electromagnetic field and pulls the cone back in. A vibration of the cone can be produced by repeatedly alternating the direction of the current. This causes the pressure in the air to vary, producing sound waves.

Page 117

1. Inducing a potential difference when a (coil of) wire cuts through the lines of force of a magnetic field.

2. Moving the magnet out of the coil.

Moving the other pole of the magnet into the coil.

3. Every half turn, a split ring commutator changes the coil connections. The connections are reversed as the induced potential is about to reverse, keeping the current flowing in one direction only.

4.

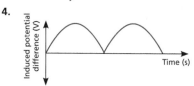

5. The diaphragm vibrates as a result of pressure variations in sound waves. These vibrations cause the coil to vibrate. A potential difference is induced as the coil moves relative to the magnetic field around the permanent magnet. A current flows as a result of the induced potential difference. The induced current changes size and direction, matching the vibrations of the coil. Electrical signals are generated from these vibrations.

Page 119

1. A device that changes electrical energy from one potential difference to another potential difference.

2.

3. Both transformers change electrical energy from one potential difference to another.

Step-up transformers increase the potential difference from the primary to the secondary coil. Step-down transformers decrease the potential difference from the primary to the secondary coil.

4. There are more turns on the secondary coil than on the primary coil in a step-up transformer.

5. a) $\dfrac{V_p}{V_s} = \dfrac{N_p}{N_s}$

$\dfrac{230}{1000} = \dfrac{50}{N_s}$

$N_s = 217$ turns

b) Step-up (as the potential difference is increased from primary to secondary)

6. $V_p I_p = V_s I_s$

So $I_p = \dfrac{(V_s I_s)}{V_s}$

$I_p = \dfrac{(230 \times 13)}{400\,000}$

$I_p = 7.5 \times 10^{-3}\,A$

Page 121

1. The Sun, the eight planets, the dwarf planets and moons (natural satellites)

2. The Milky Way

3. Planets are large bodies that orbit a star (the Sun in our solar system).

4. a) Jupiter; Saturn **b)** Uranus; Neptune

5. 67 000 mph

6. Nebulae

7. Hydrogen

8. 4.6 billion years old

Page 123

1. There is a balance of two forces: gravity pulling the star inwards and great temperatures within the star acting outwards.

2. A red giant

3. A white dwarf

4. A red supergiant

5. A supernova

6. A neutron star is formed as a result of the core of a medium-sized star remaining after a supernova.

7. A region where matter is so dense and the gravitational field is so strong that nothing can escape.

8. During fusion, hydrogen and helium fuse together to produce nuclei of heavier elements, including iron.

Page 125

1. Gravity

2. Speed is a scalar quantity and so only has magnitude, whereas velocity is a vector quantity and so has magnitude and direction.

3. It is constantly changing direction. Velocity is speed in a given direction so, if the direction changes, so does the velocity.

4. Centripetal force

5. The force of attraction between the Sun and the Earth is greater. This is because there is a smaller distance between the Sun and the Earth than there is between the Sun and Neptune.

6. The greater the distance from the Sun, the slower the orbital speed.

Page 127

1. Red light

2. Red-shift is the observed increase in the wavelength of light travelling from distant objects.

3. The greater the distance, the greater the amount of red-shift.

4. The greater the speed of the galaxy, the greater the amount of red-shift.

5. Its frequency decreases.

6. The idea that the universe is expanding; The universe started billions of years ago with a big bang.

7. It can be concluded that the galaxy is moving towards the observer since the light is shifted to the end of the spectrum with a shorter wavelength: the blue end of the spectrum.

Pages 128–133: Mixed questions

Pages 128–130

1. $\dfrac{2E_k}{v^2} = m$

$m = \dfrac{(2 \times 203)}{90^2}$

$m = 0.05\,kg = 50\,g$

2. $E_p = mgh$

$m = 0.25\,kg$

$E_p = 0.25 \times 9.8 \times 2.5$

$E_p = 6.125\,J = 6.1\,J$ (to 2 s.f.)

3. $P = I^2R = 5^2 \times 100$

$P = 2500\,W$

4. *Any suitable advantages, e.g.* fast start-up time; no pollutant gases emitted; water can be pumped back to the reservoir when electricity demand is low

Any suitable disadvantages, e.g. only certain locations are suitable (it often involves damming upland valleys); there must be adequate rainfall in the region where the reservoir is; very high initial capital outlay

5. $Q = It$

$I = \dfrac{Q}{t} = \dfrac{4500}{(15 \times 60)}$

$I = 5\,A$

6. $V = IR$

$\dfrac{V}{I} = R$

$R = \dfrac{230}{(0.1)} = 2300\,\Omega$

7.

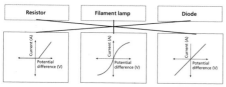

| Resistor | Filament lamp | Diode |

8. $E = Pt$

$t = \dfrac{E}{P}$

$t = \dfrac{135\,000}{900}$

$t = 150\,s$

9. The body of a car is given a negative charge and is then surrounded by its own electric field. The robotic arms control paint spray guns. The paint emitted is positively charged as it leaves the spray gun. The car's electric field pulls the positively charged paint droplets towards it, covering the car evenly. Very little paint ends up on the floor.

10.

11.

$$_{53}^{131}I \rightarrow\ _{54}^{131}Xe +\ _{-1}^{0}e$$

12. $\dfrac{\Delta E}{(mc)} = \Delta\theta$

$\Delta\theta = \dfrac{450\,000}{(2.0 \times 840)}$

$\Delta\theta = 270°C$

13. $p_1 V_1 = p_2 V_2$

$50\,000 \times 0.05 = 25\,000 \times V_2$

$V_2 = \dfrac{(50\,000 \times 0.05)}{25\,000}$

$V_2 = 0.1\,m^3$

14. Similarity *(any one from)*: each isotope has 8 protons; each isotope has 8 electrons

Difference: oxygen-16 has 8 neutrons; oxygen-17 has 9 neutrons; oxygen-18 has 10 neutrons

15. $\rho \times v = m$

$v = 0.23 \times 0.11 \times 0.08 = 2 \times 10^{-3}\,m^3$

$m = 1800 \times (2 \times 10^{-3})$

$m = 3.6\,kg$

16.

Time (minutes)	Number of nuclei remaining
0	1000
15 (after 1 half-life)	500
30 (after 2 half-lives)	250
45 (after 3 half-lives)	125
60 (after 4 half-lives)	62
75 (after 5 half-lives)	31
90 (after 6 half-lives)	15

So after $1\frac{1}{2}$ hours, there are 15 nuclei.

Pages 131–133

1. $\dfrac{W}{m} = g$

$g = \dfrac{112}{70} = 1.6\,N/kg$

2. $W = Fs$, so $s = \dfrac{W}{F}$

$F = \dfrac{500}{50} = 10\,m$

3. $v = f\lambda$

So $\lambda = \dfrac{v}{f}$

$\lambda = \dfrac{(3 \times 10^8)}{(4 \times 10^{14})} = 7.5 \times 10^{-7}\,m$

4. Force $= \dfrac{moment}{distance}$

Force $= \dfrac{20}{0.02} = 1000\,N$

Moment $=$ force $\times$ distance

Moment $= 1000 \times 0.4 = 400\,Nm$

5. $s = vt$

$v = \dfrac{s}{t}$

$v = \dfrac{15\,500}{1800} = 8.6\,m/s$

6. $a = \dfrac{(v - u)}{t}$

$u = v - at$

$u = 10 - (2 \times 3) = 4\,m/s$

7. $v = \dfrac{p}{m}$

$v = \dfrac{11\,250}{2500} = 4.5\,m/s$

8. $\sqrt{\dfrac{2Ee}{k}} = e$

$e = \sqrt{\dfrac{(2 \times 40)}{4.5}} = 4.2\,\text{m}$

9. Time taken for pulse to reach sea bed

$= \dfrac{0.8}{2} = 0.4\,\text{s}$

$s = vt$

$s = 1500 \times 0.4 = 600\,\text{m}$

10. a) Radio waves

   b) Microwaves

   c) Infrared radiation

11. Magnification $= \dfrac{\text{image size}}{\text{object size}}$

Magnification $= \dfrac{44}{5.5} = 8$

12. North to South

13. To increase the strength of the magnetic field around the coil of wire

14. Light from distant galaxies is red-shifted. The light from galaxies further away from us shows greater red-shift. This means that the further away a galaxy is from us, the faster it is moving away from us.

15. *Any one from:* move the magnet out of the coil; move the other pole of the magnet into the coil

16. a) $\dfrac{V_p}{V_s} = \dfrac{N_p}{N_s}$

$\dfrac{230}{4500} = \dfrac{100}{N_s}$

$N_s = 1957$ turns

   b) Step-up transformer as the potential difference is increased from the primary coil to secondary coil, and the number of turns is greater on the secondary coil than the primary coil.

17. The two forces are gravity, pulling the star inwards, and the radiation pressure, caused by the high temperatures due to fusion within the star, pushing it outwards.

18. If the object is travelling too fast, it will leave the orbit. If the object is travelling too slowly, it will fall to the centre of the orbit.

19. $F = BIL$

$F = 0.75 \times 13 \times 0.5$

$F = 4.9\,\text{N}$ (to 2 s.f.)

Notes

Notes